ALIGNED
To
ACHIEVE

ALIGNED

To

ACHIEVE

How to Unite Your Sales
and Marketing Teams into a
Single Force for Growth

ALIGNED
TO
ACHIEVE

Tracy Eiler
Andrea Austin

WILEY

Cover design: Michael J. Freeland

Published by John Wiley & Sons, Inc., Hoboken, New Jersey.

Published simultaneously in Canada.

For general information about our other products and services, please contact our Customer Care Department within the United States at (800) 762-2974, outside the United States at (317) 572-3993 or fax (317) 572-4002.

Wiley publishes in a variety of print and electronic formats and by print-on-demand. Some material included with standard print versions of this book may not be included in e-books or in print-on-demand. If this book refers to media such as a CD or DVD that is not included in the version you purchased, you may download this material at http://booksupport.wiley.com. For more information about Wiley products, visit www.wiley.com.

Library of Congress Cataloging-in-Publication Data:

Names: Eiler, Tracy, author. | Austin, Andrea, author.
Title: Aligned to achieve : how to unite your sales and marketing teams into
  a single force for growth / Tracy Eiler, Andrea Austin.
Description: Hoboken : Wiley, 2016. | Includes index.
Identifiers: LCCN 2016031021 (print) | LCCN 2016035377 (ebook) | ISBN
  9781119291756 (hardback) | ISBN 9781119291794 (pdf) | ISBN 9781119291770
  (epub)
Subjects: LCSH: Marketing. | Selling. | BISAC: BUSINESS & ECONOMICS /
  Marketing / General.
Classification: LCC HF5415 .E445 2016 (print) | LCC HF5415 (ebook) | DDC
  658.3/044–dc23
LC record available at https://lccn.loc.gov/2016031021

Printed in the United States of America.
10 9 8 7 6 5 4 3 2 1

To my parents, Bob and Jean, who nurtured my passion for living and learning.

—Andrea

In honor of my mom, Sandy Eiler, who taught me how to be someone who makes things happen.

—Tracy

Contents

Chapter 4

An Aligned Organization Requires a Different Kind of Leader   73

Chapter 5

Data Is the Great Equalizer of Alignment   93

Chapter 6

Push Alignment Beyond Sales and Marketing and into the CIO's Office   119

Foreword

Alignment should be the number-one operational issue for every business-to-business company. The era of fostering tension between sales and marketing is over. Businesses achieve more success and operate at a higher level—meaning more growth, more profits, and more productivity—when the teams interacting with the customer are tightly aligned. That extends from alignment on defining who the customer is, to what the customer sees and hears, to how that customer is approached, engaged with, and ultimately won.

We are in the midst of a long and unprecedented period of rapid, technology-fueled business transformation. Markets have become more competitive, products more commoditized, new business channels and methods are appearing, and technology has become ubiquitous and affordable by even the smallest companies. What that means is any company of any size can effectively compete against rivals and everyone has a harder time standing out from the growing noise in every market. Even more, buyers and buying cycles have transformed because buyers have more power and more information, which enables them to be independent of, disconnected from, and less reliant on you as a seller.

All of this has led us to today, where B2B businesses are fundamentally challenged in their go-to-market efforts. Noise in the market has skyrocketed, confusion abounds, differentiation is elusive, and buyer attention is a limited resource.

So what's a company to do?

Leaders must align their teams to focus on company growth, not departmental success. Gone are the days when sales could focus only on closing deals, marketing could focus only on generating leads, and every other department could look at their own achievements. When teams are aligned and aimed at common goals, they work better together and they win more often. But alignment is not just necessary for growth, it is necessary for survival because buyers are no longer responding to traditional and disjointed outreaches. Instead, companies must coordinate across all touchpoints where buyers are engaged, regardless of who initiates that contact or how. Buyers do not see sales and marketing; they see your brand and your company, your website and your booth at a show. Alignment enables a thoughtful, coordinated engagement with customers, and they will respond favorably.

Alignment is required, but it is not enough. It needs to be guided by a go-to-market strategy. I am starting to see a clear trend among leading companies of adopting a modern and tech-centric approach to market targeting. These companies—brands you would recognize as the most forward-thinking and innovative companies in their segments—shy away from the traditional volume approaches of outbound calls and emails. Instead they aim for quality and pinpoint targeting with the right outreach to the right person at the right time. They have learned that the old model of spray-and-pray is no longer working, so they have adopted a more focused and strategic approach.

These companies have teams that are aligned and focused, a strategic go-to-market plan, and the technologies and processes in place to execute it. As a result, they are outperforming their competitors and pulling way ahead of the others in the market. They have turned their strategy, processes, technologies, and teams into a defensible, competitive advantage for their company. It is a great time to be marketing and sales leaders, and to have the opportunity to shape the future of our companies and their revenue engines. It is also a great time to be a CEO. What is possible today wasn't even imaginable just a few years ago.

To be aligned requires leadership, and leadership begins with the CEO. It does not stop until you reach everyone in your organization. Regardless of where you fit in your company and whom you lead (even if it is just yourself), this book gives you a set of recipes that will help you break down walls, align your organization, and ensure it is ready for the challenges of going to market in this ever-evolving, complex, and challenging time. No one team can do it alone.

—Umberto Milletti
Founder and CEO, InsideView

ALIGNED
To
ACHIEVE

Why Align?

What are the topics of conversation around your office? That most likely depends on whom you talk to.

From sales reps, you probably hear complaints about low-quality leads or those that take too much nurturing to move through the sales funnel. They likely also complain that the marketing department's content does not work or is not granular enough for the specific targets, situations, or markets the sales team encounters. For example, maybe your sales reps come back from an event griping that a competitor's booth was larger, had more of a crowd, or looked better. Maybe they argue that the organization's marketing message isn't differentiated or compelling enough for them to turn opportunities into action, or that marketing is simply out of touch with the customer's needs. Your sales reps might even wonder out loud why the organization is focused on one market instead of targeting the obvious opportunity in another market.

When you talk with marketers, you probably hear their dismay that the sales department doesn't appreciate the volume of leads marketing generates and that they are too slow to follow up on hot prospects. Your marketers might mention that the content they're creating isn't being used at the right times, or at all. Maybe they express their frustration with sales reps who are too aggressive in meetings or who get preferential treatment for hitting their numbers.

Maybe marketers complain there's never enough budgeted for them to keep up with competitors. Perhaps they talk about being frustrated by not having time to create the never-ending stream of content requested by sales, or to get out in the field to visit customers and really research the market.

Does any of this sound familiar?

Think about what you're hearing from other teams within your company, or worse, from your CEO. Have they commented about the high turnover of sales reps, the missed sales forecasts, the recent loss of a major opportunity, budgets that aren't covering what's needed to win, complaints from customers, or competitors who seem to close bigger deals or have more marketing impact?

There is likely a lot of truth behind all of these complaints and the common cause is sales and marketing misalignment. The consequences of this can be dire.

Misalignment Stalls Your Path to Growth

Misalignment between sales and marketing is holding back the growth of your company—and your career.

Think about the last opportunity your organization lost and how different departments could be considered accountable. Maybe the salespeople couldn't find the content they needed, couldn't quite get the value proposition right, or couldn't articulate exactly why the customer should buy from you instead of your competitor. Marketing may not have warmed up the prospect with relevant campaigns, or may have issues with lead processing leading to lack of timely follow-up. Critical definitions and handoff points may be full of friction.

Now think about how these issues and others combine to prevent your organization from closing more business. All of those barriers to growth are caused by misalignment. According to SiriusDecisions, misalignment is to blame for companies' missing out on 19 percent faster revenue growth and 15 percent higher profitability, as shown in Figure 1.1.

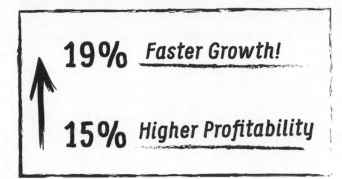

FIGURE 1.1 Aligned teams are higher-performing according to SiriusDecisions, who found that more aligned companies have significant strategic advantages over their competition.
Source: SiriusDecisions

Misalignment Leads to Mistrust and Hostility

Misalignment is rooted in the differences between how sales and marketing work, what it takes to be good at each, and how each department's success is measured. Marketers look at the big picture of markets and campaigns, while sales focuses on one deal at a time. Good sales reps are driven and aggressive, while good marketers are creative and analytical. Marketing success is based on awareness, impact, and quantities, while sales performance is measured by quota attainment.

In most organizations, sales drives revenue and marketing drives lead generation and awareness. Marketing looks at win rates and conversion rates across the sales funnel, takes the revenue target for the next quarter, and calculates how many leads are required for sales to hit their number. Sales uses the leads and content that marketing gives them and tries to close as many sales as possible.

The two departments are inherently different—from how they are compensated to how they are educated—and that's good, but it can also make it hard for sales and marketing to work together. The two teams are frequently at odds over issues as small as how to score an individual lead or as large as which markets to target. That results in mistrust, avoidance, and outright hostility between the groups, some of which is even enabled by misguided CEOs.

Get It Right: Take Those First Steps Toward Alignment

Christelle Flahaux has been a pioneer in using data to bridge marketing and sales in her senior-level roles at MapR Technologies, Jive Software, Marketo, Taleo, and Ariba. Christelle's most recent role was to sit between sales and marketing and use data to bring them into alignment. What it takes, according to Christelle, is working together and relying on data to build agreement.

"In a previous company, I discovered early on the job that our lead scoring wasn't effective," Christelle explained. "Marketing thought we were doing great because we were delivering leads that scored well, but sales complained the leads were junk. It took us a while to figure out how to do it right so we weren't delivering 20,000 marginal leads, we were delivering 3,000 good ones."

It was more than just a revamp of the lead-scoring methodology. Instead, it started a deeper conversation between marketing and sales to discover what was really important.

"We walked the sales team through our scoring methodology and discussed each and every point," Christelle continued. "What firmographic information is important? Should a tradeshow lead get more points? No. Should a white paper download get more points? Maybe. Walking through the logic helped to flesh out the thought behind it and make it transparent. It really built trust between the teams."

As they figured out the appropriate lead-scoring models, it led to more conversations and more collaboration on different items, all of which brought the teams closer to alignment.

"Eventually we talked instead of getting angry at each other," she continued. "Marketing can ask for more budget to get more leads to help sales meet their number, or we can jointly figure out how to increase close rates so sales can hire more reps. We ended up being a joint team figuring out how to meet the overall goals together."

Not getting angry at each other doesn't mean not having disagreements, however. Christelle relies on data as the key to finding a solution and avoiding lingering issues.

"If you're upset, you tend to make blanket statements, like 'We don't have any leads,'" she added. "When we rely on data, we can turn it into a fact-based conversation. We can both see exactly what's happening. Data takes the emotion out of it. It keeps you from getting defensive, especially if you approach it [by saying], 'Let's both sit down and look at the data.' It also helps you figure out what the true issues are and points you in the right direction to fix them."

Here's What We've Seen—and Why We're Devoted to Changing It

We've each been in leadership roles for more than 20 years, and we've seen our share of aligned and misaligned sales and marketing teams. We've worked under CEOs who understand the value of alignment and build a culture that fosters communication and collaboration, and we've worked under CEOs who encourage hostility between the teams, thinking that more tension yields better performance. We've also each worked with good and bad counterparts, and have learned that alignment takes commitment and work from both teams, especially their leadership.

Tracy experienced blatant misalignment firsthand when, as a newly hired SVP of marketing, she was introduced to her executive sales counterparts and they wouldn't even shake her hand. Their behavior was rude, obviously, but after watching a revolving door of marketing leaders come and go, their reasoning was sound: "You won't be around long, so why bother getting to know you?"

Andrea, as VP of sales, reached her misalignment breaking point while working with a counterpart in marketing who agreed again and again to help her out, but eventually did only what he wanted to do. When she encouraged him to work together with her on messaging improvements, he said they were just going to have to agree to disagree. What? Does that seem like reasonable progress towards alignment? No. Instead, it created a situation where marketing could take the blame if his messaging didn't work, but where he could say, "I told you so" if it did work. Andrea went about her business and found ways to work around marketing instead of *with* marketing. This undoubtedly took a toll on the company's performance, including revenue.

We've also both been exposed to the temperamental sales VPs who throw marketing under the bus every chance they get, and who always demand their way because they control the revenue. Similarly, we've all seen a weak CMO who thinks that branding is the only thing that is important. Or is myopically focused on lead-generation volumes and ignores the quality, messaging, and win rates.

Through it all, we've come to the obvious conclusion that aligned sales and marketing teams are more powerful and more productive, and create a more valuable company. Alignment also creates a more enjoyable workplace, one where marketing is challenged to perform at its best, where sales become easier, and where the entire company is aligned around one thing: growth. But alignment is hard. It's easier to live with the status quo, in the short term at least. We argue that, as a leader, you can't wait any longer. Here's why.

B2B Sales Has Changed Dramatically

Sales is difficult. First, salespeople travel—a lot. Hotels are their weekday homes, the club level is their dining room, and flight attendants know them by name.

Second, they are constantly rejected. It's not uncommon for people to hang up the phone before salespeople can get through the first sentence; that is, if anyone takes the call at all. Sales reps know that people rarely respond to their voicemails and emails. They've learned not to take it personally.

Finally, the pressure on salespeople is enormous. They're one missed quota away from unemployment. They're also responsible when a deal is lost. But this also means they can never give up; they must draw on their reserves of tenacity and resilience to try again and again. That's what has always made a good salesperson.

Until very recently, there were also some perks. Being in sales meant access to expense accounts, steak dinners, and golf outings because wining and dining was the way to win deals. Relationships trumped almost everything else and relationship building was the key to winning business.

How deals are closed today, however, is much different. Sales reps are no longer trusted advisors who are there from the beginning of the purchasing process. Thanks to the amount of information available online, prospects have more control. They do their research and consider options before sales is ever directly involved. As a result, a salesperson's role is less about building relationships and more about providing information when asked, challenging a prospect's objections, and earning the right to become an advisor.

Technology has given customers the ability to know as much about our company, our offerings, and our competitors as we do. Products are more disposable. Services are more interchangeable. Customers no longer take our word for it, and everything we say in our pitch is verified or discounted within minutes.

On the inside, each sales rep is now responsible for many more deals. Everything they do is tracked by managers and rolled up into forecasts. Promotions and demotions, opportunities and targets, are all based on *the data*, the metrics a company uses to evaluate sales performance.

On the outside, competitors have an easier time looking more successful or bigger than they truly are. They can see where you've been, where you're heading, or who you're connected to. Launching a competing offering is as easy as creating a new webpage.

In other words, sales is hard and it's getting harder. Salespeople need help—and that can come from an alignment with marketing.

B2B Marketing Has Changed Dramatically

Marketers are responsible for providing customers with the answers to the questions: *Why do anything at all? Why now? And why this company?* Marketing has to create awareness campaigns and messages that are broadly appealing yet still differentiated, and they need every customer to feel unique and special.

Until very recently, marketing was a creative role driven by gut feelings. Marketers designed advertisements, wrote brochure copy, and decided if the company logo should be printed on pens or coffee mugs. They planned events at luxury locations with big budgets. And it was easy to pump unqualified leads into the funnel simply by running another campaign.

How marketing works today, however, is much different. Data trumps gut feelings. Marketers send tens of thousands of emails in an instant, knowing only a few dozen will be opened. Pumping more leads into the pipeline doesn't matter if the lead quality is poor. Securing solid leads requires an understanding of keywords, social media, and streaming mobile video platforms.

On the inside, marketers are driven by data. They look at conversion rates and web referrals and followers and shares. They scrutinize analytics, reports, dashboards, pie charts, and traffic estimates. When they have time, they worry about the new social media sites a company does not use and the blogs where it wasn't mentioned.

On the outside, marketers find it harder to compete. Their voice is lost in a sea of noise. Bigger budgets aren't the answer to besting competitors who go viral. Existing budgets are spread across more channels and more technology, and competitors are younger, faster, and know more about us than ever before.

What remains true is that marketing exists to make sales easier. Again, it's a question of alignment.

Your Customer Has More Power and Information than You

As mentioned before, customers have become increasingly powerful. Business-to-business (B2B) sales is now, as they say, a buyer's market. For example, consider when you purchased your last car. You probably built it online first, looked at customer reviews of the model and dealerships, read articles on quality and performance, and found the dealer's invoice price so you knew exactly how much to pay. And you did all that before you even left your house.

What we've come to expect in consumer shopping—nearly complete transparency—is what we're now expecting in business transactions as well. The entire Internet is at our disposal, making it easy to find company and product reviews, scrutiny from professional bloggers and analysts, recommendations from other customers, insights from news and social media, and more. A company website provides potential customers with only a sliver of the information they can find with their own research.

There is so much readily available content that, according to CEB, an executive advisory company, nearly 60 percent of the buying process is complete before a sales rep ever gets involved. What's more, as shown in Figure 1.2, up to a third of customers in certain types of purchases would prefer not to interact with a sales rep at all. Salespeople and marketers once relied on becoming trusted advisors to their customers, but they're being quickly replaced by websites, blogs, and tweets.

For what types of purchases do you prefer to interact with a sales rep?

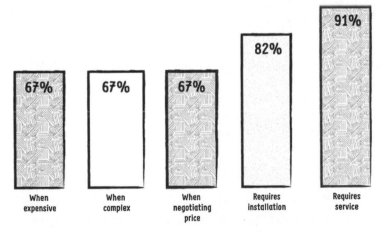

Base: 224 US B2B buyers and sellers

FIGURE 1.2 Forrester Research found that, while B2B buyers are doing far more self-guided research than ever before, they still choose to work with sales reps as purchases become more complex.

Source: Forrester Research, Inc., "Death Of A (B2B) Salesman," April, 2015.

This pivotal shift in B2B commerce has profoundly changed how sales and marketing teams must perform their craft. The old ways of selling and marketing are quickly becoming obsolete. Sales happens less often on the golf course and more in a web meeting. Marketing has less punch on a billboard and more through a tweet.

This shift is also disrupting the relationship between internal sales and marketing divisions. Marketers have to think more like sales reps, and reps have to think more like marketers. Marketing can add a "buy now" button to a website as easily and quickly as a sales rep can send a message to thousands of opportunities.

Despite this, the customer's increased ability to find information represents the critical rallying point around which sales and marketing must align. Recognizing that the customer has more power and information than ever is the first step. Sales and marketing uniting to deal with this new reality in the B2B world is the next step. This means working smarter and working together. To win, sales and marketing have to be tightly aligned in how they work, how they communicate, how they manage customers, and how they drive growth.

Misalignment Means Misunderstanding

Our marketing team at InsideView conducted an alignment survey of 1,000 B2B sales and marketing professionals (we'll dive deeper into our findings in Chapter 7). We found that neither sales nor marketing really understand what the other does.

Sales perceives marketing as being full of people who spend too much time on branding and events, trying to attract lots of eyeballs without much consideration for how they translate into revenue. Most sales reps assume that this leaves marketers out of touch with the real needs of customers.

In a year, marketing talks to only a fraction of the customers that sales talks to every day, so sales resents marketing's claim to truly know the industry and have accurate customer personas. Worse yet, marketing provides sales with their leads, but they aren't responsible for, nor measured on, pipeline or closed deals.

When marketing looks at sales, they see a bunch of mavericks driven only by quota. A marketer's perception of successful reps is that they can do whatever they want, go weeks without entering information into their customer relationship management (CRM) or other systems, and spend lavishly on expense accounts. Often, marketing thinks sales are coin-operated wheeler-dealers who are driven to find easy opportunities to put money in their pockets.

The presumptions on both sides are wrong, which becomes instantly clear if we look at how each team is measured. In our survey, we found that sales is frequently measured on much more than quota attainment. They have goals for new accounts, renewals, and upsells. We also found that two-thirds of marketers are measured on pipeline, and more than half are measured on lead *quality*.

What's apparent here is that sales and marketing are made of strikingly different personalities who continue to misunderstand each other's real roles, which are closely intertwined. But miscommunication and misperceptions don't tell the whole story. In fact, they merely scratch the surface and point to deeper, systemic issues within both teams and within most companies—and the problems are getting worse.

Get It Right: Ask Questions that Can Only Be Answered by Aligned Sales and Marketing Teams

Elisabeth Hawkins is the director of demand generation and marketing operations at PagerDuty, an operations performance platform designed to make businesses more reliable. It's a unique role that wouldn't have been thinkable just a few years ago, and it puts Elisabeth at the nexus of sales and marketing alignment. This was especially true as her company transitioned to seeking a new type of customer.

"PagerDuty was focused on smaller companies but wanted to expand to larger enterprise customers," Elisabeth explained. "It totally changed how we went to market and how our sales teams interacted with customers. We went from relying on free trials as a lead generator to working with large purchasing teams that required different content, presence at events, and complex programs that we didn't have before."

That fundamental shift in target customer brought many of their misalignment issues to the forefront, and also made it

(Continued)

(Continued)

clear that sales and marketing would need to work together if PagerDuty was going to succeed. A key decision to drive alignment was to have marketing take responsibility for revenue, not just leads.

"The strategic change in customer exacerbated all of our existing challenges," Elisabeth said. "We quickly saw that alignment was critical if we were going to scale. We also saw that marketing should be held to 100 percent of the revenue goal. Every lead encounters some sort of marketing along the way. Sales might have initiated the deal, but they'll get an email or look at some collateral eventually. Now that marketing has responsibility for revenue, they are taken more seriously by sales. It makes marketing more relevant in the eyes of the sales reps."

Once alignment started happening, it became easier for sales and marketing to quickly move beyond blame when a roadblock appeared and jump right to a discussion of solutions. Like others, including us at InsideView, lead scoring became an instant focal point.

"We wanted to get back to the basics," Elisabeth added. "We wanted a lead scoring model that everyone could understand and explain. It's also the first critical handoff between sales and marketing, so it's a great place to start working on alignment. Then it's easier to start looking at the other handoff points and hold each other accountable."

As Elisabeth and her colleagues became more aligned, data became the next obvious focus.

"We started to ask ourselves about the minimum amount of data we needed to achieve our goals," she continued. "Did we need a lead's industry and number of employees? If so, where was it going to come from? Should we automate it with a service or rely on sales to research it? These were questions that both sales and marketing had to agree upon since we were going to be heavily relying on that data. But then we started thinking about targeting, and we knew based on experience that a great lead for us was a company who was 'tech forward.'

You can't just buy that data. It's not a typical attribute you enter into a lead form."

Since the teams at PagerDuty were already well aligned by this point, it was easier to work together with the common goal of growing the business.

"It became a great conversation starter, just asking ourselves who are our best customers and why," Elisabeth added. "Having those discussions, figuring it out together, and deciding how to make it happen really brought out teams closer together."

Misalignment Is Getting Worse and Here's Why

Most sales and marketing teams are so wrapped up in their internal goals and metrics that the "customer" becomes this external, almost imaginary, entity. Sales and marketing think about generating more leads and closing more deals more often than they consider what customers want. This inward focus creates blinders that mask the real, external forces that are causing further fractures and divergence in how sales and marketing work together.

Technology Broke Down Silos and They Grew Back

In the 2000s, enterprise software was the end all, be all to your B2B ills. One of the key benefits, according to software vendors, was the elimination of silos of data created by legacy systems. The promise: Put all of your data into our system and finance can see sales forecasts, customer service can see billing issues, and sales can see marketing touch points. It was a great concept and it worked. But now, with cloud-based tools and new channels popping up, it's easier than ever to add new software tools as you attempt to keep pace.

In a nutshell, here's what has happened: You have too much technology, you have too much data, and everything is constantly changing. It creates distractions and silos, which exacerbate misalignment. We'll dive deeper into this in Chapters 5 and 6.

The Boundary Between Sales and Marketing Is Blurry

Largely due to technology, sales reps and marketers are stepping into each other's role more and more and their tasks are converging. Add to this the extreme level of miscommunication or lack of communication entirely and you have *both* sales and marketing doing what's best for themselves instead of collaborating on what's best for the customer and the company's growth.

For instance, if a sales rep wants to invite 25 prospects to an event to find more opportunities, they do it without including marketing. Meanwhile, if marketing wants to start working on the automotive market to get more prospects, they do it without any input from sales. Sure, they each might give the other a heads-up, but the focus on remaining independent keeps both groups from considering the full impact of what they're doing and how it affects the other—or the customer.

Your Current Success Shouldn't Fool You

Right now you may be thinking something like, "Well, things are going pretty well at my company without all of this alignment stuff." Think again. Industry analyst IDC claims that a lack of sales and marketing alignment can cost you 10 percent of your revenue. *Ten percent!* Think about what an extra 10 percent in revenue could mean for your company. A study by marketing automation provider Marketo found that well-aligned teams have win rates 30 percent higher. *Thirty percent!* What would a 30 percent higher win rate have meant for your company last quarter?

You might be perfectly content to stick with your current business process, keeping sales focused on closing deals and marketing focused on filling the funnel. But before you decide to take no action, consider the benefits of sales and marketing alignment: You could increase revenue, profitability, win rates, and more. Why wouldn't you align? Compared to the performance of an aligned organization, your current success isn't actually all that great. We asked Jim Dickie, former managing partner at CSO Insights, a sales and marketing effectiveness research firm, why all companies aren't jumping on the alignment bandwagon.

"I honestly don't know," Jim says. "This should be a boardroom-level discussion. It's that important. Our research is showing that B2B win rates are steadily declining and are now around 47 percent, on average. That's terrible. The odds of winning at the craps tables in Las Vegas are 49 percent, so companies would be better off gambling!"

Jim says that companies think too much about how much it costs to drive alignment and not enough about the price they pay for resisting change. "The cost of doing nothing is magnitudes higher than of doing something," Jim added. "When I see companies doing nothing, it makes me cringe."

What It Takes to Align

Let us define alignment by pointing to a metric of *misalignment*. In our survey of 1,000 sales and marketing professionals, we asked them this question: How often do you meet with the other team to discuss pipeline? As you can see in Figure 1.3, nearly two-thirds of sales said *quarterly or less*. More than three-quarters of marketing said *monthly or more*. That's quite a discrepancy. We can't imagine anyone is lying, so how can they be so out of sync?

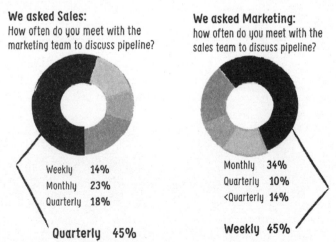

We asked Sales:
How often do you meet with the
marketing team to discuss pipeline?

Weekly   14%
Monthly   23%
Quarterly 18%

Quarterly   45%

We asked Marketing:
how often do you meet with the
sales team to discuss pipeline?

Monthly   34%
Quarterly   10%
<Quarterly 14%

Weekly   45%

FIGURE 1.3 Simply meeting to discuss pipeline resulted in widely different answers from sales and marketing teams.

Source: Demand Gen Report and InsideView Inc., "Cracking the Code of Sales & Marketing Alignment," February, 2016

The roots of misalignment stem from such fundamental issues as communication and perceptions, but it's so much more than that.

Alignment means creating a common focus and putting everything behind it. In this book, we'll make the case for why pipeline must be the focal point, why data must be the foundation for alignment, and why growth must be the common thread.

We're not advocating for the end of marketing and sales as we know it. We believe they are two distinct teams with two distinct roles that require two very distinct skill sets. We see alignment as turning these two teams into a collaborative, focused unit racing towards the same goal.

Sales and marketing alignment isn't easy. But putting growth at the center of your efforts gets everyone focused on the same point. It becomes the central goal around which an aligned company can be built.

Face It: You're Codependent

InsideView's CEO, Umberto Milletti, likes to say that the sales and marketing relationship is a codependency. Both teams need each other to succeed.

It's almost expected for sales to market and marketing to stay engaged closer to the contract signing. Buyers are choosing their own paths, so they interact on a whim and follow their own process, not the one your company has set. Alignment helps organizations adapt because there will be more collaboration, more handoffs, and more blurring of lines between the two teams.

"CMOs have to understand much more about the entire revenue process than ever before," Umberto explains. "Much more than just lead flow, but even into the granular challenges sales reps have in converting pipeline into revenue. In the other direction, sales VPs have to think about and understand the marketing activity that moves deals through the funnel."

The aligned organization means that both teams are reliant on each other, so those with combative approaches are going to have a difficult time. If sales thinks they are in charge, they will get less collaboration from marketing.

"Sales is more dependent on marketing, so they have to have less of a cowboy mentality," Umberto continues. "That won't work long term. Sales absolutely needs marketing to be successful." But just as with any modern relationship, if it's not working out, both teams are often more willing to call it quits than try to work out a cooperative solution.

"I've seen sales executives be much quicker to say, 'This CMO isn't working,'" added Umberto. "They used to just write marketing off, stop working with them. Now they will push for a change in leadership. Marketing does the same if they see that their hard work isn't turning into revenue or they don't see the necessary talent downstream in sales. Those CMOs are pushing harder because they are measured on pipeline."

Alignment takes a good deal of understanding of each other's roles, challenges, and actions. Both sales and marketing rely on the other for high performance. Both teams have to be willing to work together, and they also have to realize that they're ultimately accountable. If your people are not holding up their end of the relationship, their days may be numbered.

To be clear, aligning sales and marketing isn't some feel-good effort. Tight alignment pays tangible, higher-value dividends. Operationally, we're talking about things like improving prospecting results, higher lead-conversation and sales-win rates, lower customer-acquisition costs, and increased productivity among marketing and sales teams. Strategically, it gets even better: faster close rates, improved customer retention and expansion, better understanding and targeting of a company's best customers, and a widening of total addressable market.

Ultimately, we believe sales and marketing alignment opens the door for a new and shared vision that represents a better way forward. It also means getting back to the basics and working together to set shared goals and move toward common outcomes.

What to Expect from This Book

In this book we'll show you how to prepare your company for alignment, how to get the leadership behind it, and how to get both sales and marketing on board. We'll detail why data must be the foundation of any successful alignment initiative, and we'll explain how to use the four pillars of alignment (leadership, culture, process, and technology; see Figure 1.4) to your advantage.

We'll also show you how to overcome objections and avoid mistakes along the way. Throughout the book you will find case studies from companies who have taken on the challenge of alignment.

As preparation to write this book, we interviewed over 50 respected sales and marketing thought leaders and pored over hundreds of articles and analyst reports on sales and marketing alignment. In addition to *our* thoughts and research, we'll also share tips from these leaders and insights from noted experts and analysts.

Let's go!

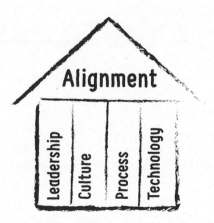

FIGURE 1.4   Alignment is built only with the support of great culture, process, leadership, and technology.

Get Those Cultural Obstacles out of Your Way

Sales and marketing alignment is a call for radical change, and radical change requires a company culture that is adaptable, resilient, and flexible. It also requires a base level of willingness—willingness to collaborate, to communicate, to be respectful, and to put the shared goals of sales and marketing at the forefront of everything you do.

We like to think of sales and marketing as the tip of the spear. We are the first to engage with the customer, whether it's sales or marketing, and whether it's an inbound or outbound effort. Sales and marketing are the first touch points a customer has with your company. By thinking of united sales and marketing as the tip of the spear, you can begin to imagine how the rest of your company can align behind them. There is nothing more important to your organization than growth. Building a culture that aligns behind your growth drivers is an absolute requirement for success.

Alignment Must Be a CEO-Driven Initiative

InsideView's CEO, Umberto Milletti, stated in the introduction that alignment should be a CEO's number-one operational issue. It is a clear path to increased revenue growth, which is the CEO's job. We're lucky to work as the sales and marketing leaders under such a visionary CEO, and we're not just saying that because we report to him.

We both started at InsideView independently. Andrea was first on board and the company had the typical sales and marketing relationship. It was not great, but it was not terrible, either. When Tracy joined just over a year later, creating a tighter alignment between sales and marketing was one of her directives from day one.

"Traditionally, sales and marketing have been very independent," says Umberto. "The evolution of the marketplace has created more and more competition and the blurring of sales and marketing roles. But from the CEO's point of view, we can see the *strategic* blurring. I saw that marketing was getting more involved in revenue creation. I saw that sales was reaching out earlier in the process and doing some marketing on their own. And I recognized that, even though customers generally first engage with marketing, their first experience with a *person* is with sales. So, from my view in the CEO's seat, creating a tightly aligned customer experience across sales and marketing touchpoints was becoming even more important, especially in our competitive market."

From *our* seats, as sales and marketing executives, we agree that it would be very difficult, if not impossible, to drive alignment without the complete support of the CEO. Support means the CEO sees it as a differentiator, a key driver of growth, and a key component of the company's overall strategy.

Only the CEO can create a culture that is supportive of alignment.

BVR Mohan Reddy is founder and executive chairman of Cyient, a global engineering services firm headquartered in Hyderabad, India. Running such a large organization across countries and cultures—Cyient has more than 12,800 associates across 38 global locations—increases both the chances for misalignment and the need for strong CEO guidance supporting it.

"We're continually looking at improving sales and maximizing investor value," Mohan says. "In doing so, we're looking for gaps and places where we can do better. We don't see sales and marketing as discrete departments. They are components of a company that is totally focused on generating revenue. Alignment of them is driven by the CEO, not by sales and not by marketing."

Mohan boils their alignment philosophy down to three specific areas: communication, process, and technology.

"Open and clear communication is critical," Mohan explains. "It's true in any organization. The CEO has to be the leader in displaying open communication. Process is equally important. When you lay out a clearly defined process, friction is minimized. And, you need good technology to make it all happen, and there needs to be conformity in your technology. Technology should be looked at as a solution for the company, not a sales solution or a marketing solution. Since revenue generation is a company initiative, as is alignment, the CEO must be the driver in all of these areas."

These are two instances of a CEO successfully creating a culture where alignment can occur. But let's look at it from the opposite perspective: The CEO can also create a culture where *misalignment* is encouraged.

Tension Does Not Belong on the Path to Alignment

We've both worked at companies where the teams were not aligned, and we assume you have, too. In some cases, the CEOs of these companies felt that tension between sales and marketing would yield the best performance and drive the best effort. Of course, a level of healthy tension is always good, and it holds people accountable. But building a culture of combative tension is unhealthy, and can border on abusive. More experienced sales and marketing executives will run from that type of culture, and we recommend that you do, too!

"I am the type of CEO who puts a high level of value on respect and open communication," says Umberto. "I do not like fighting or back-stabbing. That is definitely not OK in my organization."

Tracy had an experience at a former company where, after just a few weeks as CMO, she found some major holes in their lead-to-close reporting. Essentially, the company had a major problem with duplicate leads, which inflated their top-of-funnel metrics. After more digging, she found even more discrepancies in their data. When she presented her findings to the CEO—who had based the company's reputation and fund-raising strategy on their stellar conversion rates—he shut her down. It was an emperor-has-no-clothes moment. Tracy recognized the writing on the wall and, not long after that, she left the company. The CEO had created a culture where it was not OK to talk about problems in the open, especially ones that were particularly impactful.

Working toward alignment is going to bring up dozens of challenges, roadblocks, and screeching-brake moments. This is all part of the process *and* half of the benefit of alignment: uncovering the problems that are holding back your growth. But getting beyond these problems and recognizing them as opportunities requires a culture of patience, openness, and collaboration. And that's just to start.

What is important to remember is that alignment is a form of professional development and organizational evolution. You're turning your teams into *high-performing teams*, and your organization into a *high-performing organization*.

As sales and marketing start working more closely and nosing around in each other's business and processes, you're undoubtedly going to find mistakes, errors, and outright questionable decision-making that creates tension on both sides. Often those issues are simply based on processes not having changed as your business changed.

Respect is the key. You are not going to make progress by throwing colleagues under the proverbial bus or pointing fingers. You're collaboratively trying to move forward and it takes mutual respect to look beyond the past and toward the future.

"A culture of respect is very important to me," says Umberto. "The downside of respect is that it can be interpreted as needing to always 'be nice' or to not call people out on their errors. It happens everywhere, including InsideView, but having respect for a person also means being direct and honest. You can be respectful and professional but still call someone out on missing a deadline."

When a CEO is leading the alignment charge, and when the culture is more focused on improvements and growth, finger-pointing and unhealthy tension become unnecessary and, eventually, irrelevant.

Culture Is Scalable

Alignment is a facilitator of growth. You're not just doing this for fun, but to help your organization grow faster. As that happens, your company has to scale to support changes that come with increased size, budgets, and so on. That means hiring people, expanding your reach, and more.

Luckily, culture can scale, too. It extends far beyond just sales and marketing, and helps everyone in your company understand the need for a project as big as sales and marketing alignment. It also helps everyone get behind the alignment and do what's needed to support it. Human Resources will understand the need to look for collaborators over individual executors. Finance will understand the need to budget for tools and programs that streamline alignment. A culture of collaboration empowers people to work together rather than do their work and just throw things over the wall to the next team.

Unfortunately, however, you can't plan and design a great culture at the individual employee level. The CEO has to provide the guiding principles, and the other executives need to constantly reinforce the importance of that culture to the wider company. As the organization grows, an effective culture continues to reflect those guiding principles and ensures that everyone (including new hires) stays true to them.

Every role in your company is inevitably crossfunctional, so an inward focus tends to affect another team for better or worse. For example, marketing impacts sales, but also HR (what candidates find when they research your company), customer service (what customers expect from your company), and alliances (what other companies think of your company and its offerings). Other teams have their part to play, as well. To understand how customer service impacts HR, think of your last appointment with the cable company and ask yourself if that is the kind of place you want to work. A good culture is one in which the focus is not inward, but is instead on the customer and what is best for the entire organization.

"Having a great culture extends to every employee and helps guide their decision-making," added Umberto. "If you have a customer-focused culture, every decision will be made based on what's best for customers, and customers will recognize it and reward you for it."

Alignment Forces You to Move beyond Blame

As we mentioned, when you begin to align your teams, you're going to find lots of errors, missed handoffs, inconsistencies, and more. How you react is what will make or break your success. By *react*, we mean how you treat each other at the tactical level.

Questions like "Who did this?" are rarely helpful and don't usually lead to a solution. But questions like "What impact is this having?" and "What is the history behind this decision?" and "How can we fix this?" can help you begin to find solutions.

Your goal is to develop a shared attitude where you want to learn from the past, and where you realize that your fully aligned teams will be able to make better decisions and perform at a higher level. But attitude can only take you so far. Andrea has a pet peeve: When her team repeats the same mistakes over and over again, she loses her patience. This is where you have to move beyond blame and start to focus on direct and honest communication. That's why you're the leader and, in those situations, you need to step up and set clear expectations.

If you're an executive, you might run the risk of your team, and even your peers, thinking that your alignment initiative is just a shiny new diversion. They might see you as the latest CMO with crazy new ideas that'll quickly change once the reality of your business rears its head. Or they might think that, as VP of sales, your focus on alignment will disappear a month into the next week or quarter. Or, they might choose to just wait you out and see what happens because you might not be around very long. Executive turnover is especially acute in the tech industry, where the CMO and VP of sales both have an average tenure of *less than two years*. In other industries, it's a bit better, with *Forbes* reporting that CMOs, can expect a four-year run, on average.

Remember Tracy's story about her executive sales counterparts refusing to shake her hand? It was the short tenure of her predecessors that prompted them to assume she wouldn't be around long so there was no need to put any effort into her initiatives.

In the right culture, the entire company will recognize the importance of alignment and rally behind it. *Sales will know that they can't succeed alone. Marketing will know they exist to make sales easier. And alignment won't be seen as the latest initiative from the latest CMO.* Remember those lines because we'll refer back to them frequently. It's a kind of mantra we like to repeat to remember how we must work together.

Recognize Your Differences as You Build Your Alignment Strategy

As with any initiative, sales and marketing alignment begins with your leadership team. Getting sales and marketing on board is, of course, also critical.

First, let's recognize that sales and marketing are two distinct roles. The roles are blurring, for sure, and there's Forrester Research principal analyst Andy Hoar, in their April 2015 "Death Of A (B2B) Salesman" report, predicting that "1 million, or just over 20% of all B2B salespeople, will be displaced by self-serve eCommerce by 2020." But in reality, sales and marketing aren't going away nor are they being morphed into one department.

We've talked about the distinct differences between what's required to be a good sales rep versus a good marketer. Andrea likes to say that she looks for "control freaks" when she's hiring new reps. On the other hand, Tracy looks for "creative collaborators" when hiring marketers. Those traits are polar opposite and rarely found in the same person. No wonder these teams have trouble seeing eye-to-eye.

"The people who do well in sales versus marketing are very different," adds Umberto. "A great sales leader is tactical, and very near-term focused, so not the person you want running your marketing team. A great CMO is visionary, strategic, and likes to think things through. Those are great traits for each role, but it also leads to difficulties in getting them to work together and communicate."

Marketing, however, has to be comfortable seeing sales as their customer. Just as dicey, but it serves as the basis for a collaborative relationship, sales has to see marketing as their enabler. Andrea frequently tells her team they can lose alone, but they cannot win alone, so leverage your extended team.

Tracy says again and again that "marketing exists to make sales easier." And she qualifies this by saying, "Marketers aren't a bunch of doormats." They don't just take orders from the sales team.

As CMO Kim DeCarlis of Imperva says, "Marketing serves sales, but we aren't servants. It's important to establish the subtleties of this dynamic early in the relationship and at every level. Bringing insights and ideas to the table that impact revenue, and actively discussing and trying ideas together can set the foundation for a long-standing partnership between the groups."

This relationship dynamic is an important one to agree to and drive through the culture of the organization. And the attitude that marketing is clearly serving sales, and sales cannot succeed alone, must start with the leadership.

Get Teams on Board or out of the Way

Both sales and marketing leaders must have the right perspective and believe in alignment. It can't be just talk. And it might require a few personnel changes early on.

Personalities are critical and those of the leadership have to fit the alignment mold. They have to see each other as partners, not enemies. It is important to ensure that the sales and marketing leaders have the right personalities and an equally strong desire to become aligned. The CEO needs to assess both the talent and mindset of the executive team and across the company because both of those aspects are important. Great talent that won't collaborate is bad. Your leaders have to model the right behavior and their teams have to emulate them.

Unfortunately, some people won't fit within an aligned company. That's OK. It's better for them to move on to a place where they can thrive—and it's better for you to encourage them to move on so as not to be a drag on your efforts.

The Sales Psyche

Why Sales Is Responsible for Their Own Destiny

John Barrows provides customized sales training and consulting services to top B2B brands, and he has worked with thousands of sales reps over the years. He has watched as B2B selling has rapidly evolved, and he's noticed what separates those who want to survive from those who are struggling to hang on. While a lot of that evolution revolves around technology, it also requires acceptance that the sales role is changing.

"I'm 40, so I'm roughly in the middle, seeing the sides of both new and old reps" says John. "I see older sales reps understand that technology is critical and they won't survive without getting on board. And I'm seeing the younger generation of reps who use lots of tech, but they don't have the selling skills to make it work. It's indicative of the changing nature of sales, and of business. It's forcing sales to look to marketing for assistance, which is both helping *and* hurting alignment."

With sales and marketing roles evolving so quickly, due to technology but also competition, and with the changing buyer, and other factors, John sees sales starting to lose ground to marketing in the race for relevance.

"Marketing is evolving so much faster than sales," John says. "The value of both of our roles is being diminished, because technology is able to do so much more, but sales isn't adapting as quickly as marketing. It's creating a digital divide and it is forcing sales to rely much more on marketing."

While sales' reliance on marketing is good for marketing, it's not always good for alignment. Sales wants marketing to work better for them, but they don't speak the same language as marketing and their expectations are misaligned.

"There's a difference between what sales wants from marketing and what sales *should* want from marketing," John adds. "Sales wants very qualified leads and a pre-scheduled meeting with someone who is already interested in buying. That's just ludicrous. Sales should want more relevant content, more

(Continued)

(*Continued*)

content focused on specific personas, more messaging they can use in real conversations. Marketing is great at providing awareness and branding and inbound leads, but once a prospect says 'let's talk,' marketing goes silent. Marketing doesn't get that sales needs something to work with when a prospect does finally pick up the phone. But it's somewhat sales' fault, too."

Ultimately, John says, sales has to take responsibility for not only supporting alignment but for holding up their end of the bargain.

"I think marketing should spend all of their time on case studies," John says, only partially in jest. "Talk to a customer once in a while. Seriously though, it's really up to sales to make the introductions, to do a better job of helping marketing succeed. For something like measuring impact, sales should be gathering data during every deal to build ROIs or figure out a way to measure impact. I know they are asking the questions, so why not hand a list of metrics to marketing once a deal closes?"

"Sales should see alignment as a clear benefit to themselves," John added. "Back in the old days, sales was an art form. You either had it or you didn't. Same with marketing. But now they are both a science. Marketing is already getting it, but sales isn't."

For sales reps, John has one piece of final advice: "Marketing is slowly taking over your job. If you don't get aligned, you're gonna get replaced."

Tenets of an Alignment Culture

To build your alignment culture, as we've mentioned before, you have to focus on collaboration. You also need to align your company around growth and serving the customer. Finally, data and metrics need to be in place to track your progress and keep sales and marketing focused on growth and the right goals.

Collaboration

Collaboration is the backbone of alignment. There needs to be an environment where people are not only encouraged to work together, but they also *want* to work together. There's a distinction there that is rooted in culture and how it impacts your hiring process.

In our survey of sales and marketing professionals, we found that, even though they sometimes misunderstand and misrepresent each other, there is a strong sense of comradery that helps foster alignment. Our survey found that more than two-thirds of those on the marketing and sales teams consider themselves friends of people on the other team. Unfortunately, our survey also found the number-one challenge to alignment is communication, which is a cornerstone of collaboration. Ultimately, sales and marketing have to do more than just work together. True collaboration means being involved with each other, jointly setting and working toward goals, and constantly communicating.

From a cultural standpoint, we like to tell our teams at Inside-View to "seek to understand." Marketing needs to understand how sales works, how reps are measured, and the challenges that they face with customers. Sales needs to understand the same of marketing. It's also important that both teams understand reporting relationships, sales methodologies, how leads are scored, and what customers are saying. Without a culture that supports this level of transparency, collaboration won't happen. Without collaboration, alignment will fail to reach its potential, and potentially fail altogether.

Growth, Handoffs, and the Customer Experience

Understanding your funnel and how customers traverse it is critical to both alignment and the customer experience, which directly impacts growth. Having tangible metrics helps identify bumps along the way. As customers bounce back and forth between sales and marketing touchpoints, these handoffs are where trouble usually occurs.

"CEOs should focus on conversions from one step to the next in the customer journey," Umberto recommends. "That's where the handoffs happen, so poor metrics will point to bad handoffs. It could be poor communication. It could be conflicting tactics. But conversion rates will show you where the customer journey is falling apart."

Handoffs are critical to the customer experience, organizational growth, and sales and marketing alignment. Think about it from the perspective of a restaurant server giving a dinner order to a member of the kitchen staff. That's a critical handoff that directly impacts the customer experience and influences their decision to return or recommend the restaurant to friends. If the waiter leaves out information, doesn't capture the order correctly, or doesn't put it in the correct spot, those mistakes will make their way to the customer. The kitchen may cook the wrong items, prepare them incorrectly, or not complete an order. The same can be said of marketing handing a lead to sales. If the customer was interested in product X, but that detail was missing from the handoff, then sales might pitch them instead on product Y and fail to understand their needs.

Poor handoffs negatively impact the customer experience. And that poor experience impacts success, which impacts growth. "In my experience, almost all of your customer issues are happening at handoff points," adds Umberto.

With a growth- and customer-focused culture, sales and marketing have a shared rallying point. When conflict arises, the discussion isn't around what's best for sales or what's best for marketing. It always comes back to what's best for the customer in order to support growth. In some cases, it might be adding a customer communication channel. In other cases, it might require changes to a sales or marketing process.

Your fundamental relationship with your customers is also changing, moving from a won-and-done relationship to an ongoing partnership. It requires a cultural shift to get both sales and marketing to continue thinking about the customer long after the contract has been signed.

"The B2B selling approach has changed into a long-term relationship," says John Kelly, InsideView's chief revenue officer, who has more than 20 years of executive sales experience. "In the past, reps sold to a customer and didn't care if they ever used the product. Now, in many industries, you're selling to that customer every day, getting them to use the product, buy more of it, buy other products. It's a cultural shift for the entire company because you're continually selling. It's the CEO who sets that culture, and it has to come from the top."

Data and Metrics

We'll cut right to the point: We believe that pipeline is absolutely the most important metric for sales and marketing alignment, and that's a major cultural shift for most companies.

Let's back up a moment and define *pipeline*. Pipeline refers to the opportunities the sales team believes could convert into revenue. This is different from leads, people who have expressed very early interest, because pipeline holds actual opportunities that are qualified through both the marketing and sales process.

Pipeline is what forecasts and drives your revenue. If you have more deals of higher value in the pipeline, that indicates more eventual revenue. Pipeline is uniquely impacted by both sales and marketing. You might be thinking, "Marketing doesn't close deals, they only generate leads." It is true that marketing doesn't close deals. But they are responsible for the *quality* of the leads generated, and making sure they turn into actual opportunities. Many marketing teams feel their responsibility ends with the lead handoff. In a truly aligned organization, marketing sees leads through until they are qualified by sales and creates an opportunity. Marketing also pays attention to the ultimate outcome, of winning or losing that deal, and the reasons why.

Let's say marketing only generates leads that have low values. For example, if marketing contributes lots of small deals to the pipeline, then sales has to close more of them to reach their goals. It's also possible that marketing contributes weak leads to the pipeline. In that case, win rates fall and sales, again, has to work more leads to reach their goals or take time to find their own leads.

In this discussion of metrics, we're zeroing in on marketing because they are the ones that need to be convinced that they have a role beyond lead generation and must be involved in the entire pipeline. Everyone in sales already knows they're responsible for pipeline. In marketing, it's a tougher sell. Most marketers will say, "I can control lead generation, but I can't control whether sales can turn that into pipeline." We argue that marketing has a lot of influence on whether leads become pipeline. Lead quality is only one dimension. The right content, sales enablement, and process are also factors. Marketing must embrace their responsibility for pipeline if your organization wants to reap the benefits of alignment.

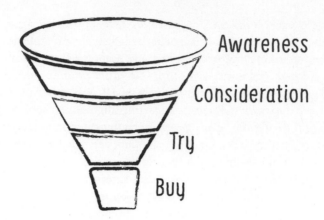

FIGURE 2.1   A simplified version of the typical sales funnel, where marketing is responsible for the top and sales for the bottom.

Pipeline alignment gives both sales and marketing a stronger stake in the company's success. Marketing can't hide behind excuses like, "Sales isn't doing their job." Pipeline will show both teams what they need to do to hit their targets (Figure 2.1). Maybe sales needs to improve their close rates, but the issue might be that marketing is overselling your offering or bringing in leads that aren't a good fit.

On the one hand, we recommend that marketing be measured on other traditional sales metrics, like the aforementioned win rates as a measure of lead quality. What metrics you choose will be unique to your business, but they should help get marketing more aligned with what sales needs from them.

On the other hand, sales can have a direct impact on marketing's performance. While we believe marketing exists to make sales easier, that doesn't mean that marketing follows sales around with an order form. We need sales to follow up on leads, collaborate on programs, and weigh in on process. Sales must be invested in marketing's success. If marketing needs help with market feedback, listening in on customer calls, or building awareness for an event, sales should be not only willing but also eager to help. The better marketing performs, the better sales performs. They are codependent—in a good way!

This seems a bit one sided (in sales' favor) but, once again, it all comes back to culture. If your company is flexible and collaborative, and has a focus on doing what's best for growth, marketing will see the value in being measured on pipeline and other revenue-side metrics.

We'll admit it's going to be a tough sell. We've both spoken at many events aimed at sales and marketing alignment. We frequently take an informal show-of-hands poll of audiences, asking marketers if they are measured on pipeline. Without fail, very few hands are raised. And the look on people's faces is often either confusion or outright skepticism. It's a scary prospect for marketers, but having the right cultural foundation will ease the transition.

We'll talk later about adding pipeline goals to your marketing team's compensation package. That's when you'll really shake things up! But the benefits are worth it.

A Way to Measure Trust

Megan Heuer, vice president of research at SiriusDecisions, recently wrote about the lack of trust between sales and marketing, and how critical a shared trust is to execution. But how do you measure trust? You can ask your team members if they trust others, but as the saying goes, "Actions speak louder than words."

How do you know if trust is lacking? For marketers, we recommend this (decidedly non-scientific) checklist to determine if sales trusts them when they go forward with a change. Megan offered it to us and we think it's great.

How many of these statements could you or your team answer affirmatively today?

- Will a salesperson (rep or leader) take a call or meeting with you or is he or she always too busy?
- Does sales respond to your email requests? Do salespeople provide feedback if asked?
- Does sales invite you (or allow you if you ask) to join any of their meetings?
- Does sales allow you to join them on prospect or customer calls if you ask?
- Will the salesperson allow you to see an account plan?

- Does sales use the information or tools you provide to them?
- Does sales follow up on the leads you send, even if it's to reject them?
- Will a salesperson share an account plan with you if you ask?
- Do you know what most salespeople would say if you asked them what they thought marketing did to help their productivity? Would you like the answer?

Megan says, "All of these questions offer clues to marketing's current level of emotional permission to make changes and execute." Ultimately, she added, if marketing makes a mistake, "it's the salesperson who can lose out on the source of his or her livelihood." If your paycheck relied even partially on someone else's actions, you'd be darn sure you trusted them.

Get Ready for These Common Objections to Alignment

Once you have a culture that can support alignment, the rest is easy, right? Definitely not! Both sales and marketing will have resistance to alignment, from the CMO down to the field sales reps. Here's an overview of the common objections you're likely to hear, and what you can do to change minds.

We've both been sales and marketing leaders long enough to have transitioned ourselves and our teams through these objections many times. What's important is to keep the focus on the facts, which is where data comes in, and the customer, which is where culture comes in.

What Is Marketing Afraid Of?

Sales' expectations of marketing are completely unrealistic—and they always will be. Sales is never satisfied. They want to blow out their quota and they want it to be easy. Even when marketing is doing well and working long hours, sales will still want more.

Alignment won't stop sales from dreaming of a world where one phone call nets them a million-dollar deal every time. What alignment will do is make them more realistic about pipeline.

Visibility into marketing programs and conversion rates—the data—can help here. Getting sales involved earlier in campaigns and strategies, then following up with results later will help them understand how the pipeline is filled by marketing and how quality is affected. It starts with how much pipeline coverage the sales team needs. A historical rule of thumb is you need a pipeline three-times your revenue goal in order to meet that goal. That means only one-third of the pipeline will close, but that coverage metric really varies by customer target, industry, and more. It is critical for marketing to understand the coverage requirements and sign up for realistic pipeline goals based on their program efforts and budgets, and the sales team's ability to convert opportunities into deals.

Sales Won't Follow Up on Leads So Marketing's Time and Money Will Be Wasted

Marketers knows that sales is a tough, demanding, pressure-filled world. Sometimes, however, when they look at the data, they see piles of leads that sales never contacted. That might be because sales didn't record some follow-up activity into their customer relationship management (CRM) system. In part, it could also be because sales disqualified certain leads for whatever reason. Consistent and comprehensive data is critical here, if only to let marketing know that follow-up is happening.

The real challenge comes because marketing often declares success when large volumes of leads come in, but they become frustrated when sales misses their goals. Alignment will bring marketing and sales closer together, which will allow marketers to better understand both why leads aren't being contacted (e.g., "not one lead from that event was interested, so I stopped calling them") and why close rates aren't what anyone is expecting.

Sales Is Constantly Distracted; They Don't Listen, Only Complain

You're working on collaboration, right? Your marketing team is listening to sales, right? They are seeking to understand each other, right? This objection goes back to the foundation of culture and alignment that both teams need to be open to. That might mean that marketing has to work for a tighter bond with sales by really listening to their complaints and digging deeper, asking questions, and discovering the root cause of them. Maybe when someone says, "All of those event leads are garbage," what he really means is that your lead-scoring system needs some work or the definition of a qualified lead has to change.

Sales Doesn't Appreciate What Marketing Does for Them

Sales reps can have a "what have you done for me lately" attitude. They frequently want fresh leads, not ones that entered the cycle a year ago. They expect marketing to deliver, no matter the cost or the effort, yet they rarely offer any appreciation for the final results.

In most cases sales doesn't appreciate the results of marketing's work because they don't understand what goes into a specific activity. They may think that an email campaign is just a few clicks in a marketing automation tool, or that a field event requires just a few phone calls and a menu. Educating sales counterparts on the people-hours required for different types of campaigns will help them really understand the efforts needed to pull off their requests. We've found that a webinar takes 40 to 60 hours of effort to produce. The average sales rep probably has no idea that much time is involved. Bring sales reps into the planning process of a campaign early so they can appreciate the level of detail and the amount of work required. It's important to show the sales team how marketing is load-balancing their work, and explain the cost of each program in money and especially in time.

Sales Doesn't Put the Right Information into the CRM and Other Systems

When working toward alignment, everyone has to be flexible and change in some way. You're going to encounter a lot of people saying, "We've always done it this way" or "No one cares about that piece of data." Transparency and data sharing can help to overcome these excuses. Maybe sales was never educated on the value certain data has for marketing, or perhaps marketing never explained to sales how certain data can help them provide better, bigger, or higher-quality leads. Using data as the foundation of alignment (see Chapter 5) and working together on defining what data is important *and why* will help everyone understand the data's value.

It's Not Fair to Measure Marketing on the Sales Pipeline

This is the big objection from marketers, without a doubt, but being measured on pipeline is critical to alignment success. It's still a new concept, however, so it may take some time. When you suggest tying compensation to pipeline, it can make marketers scared. To overcome this, remind the marketing team that marketing exists to make sales easier. Contributing to a larger pipeline with better conversion rates is how marketing measures their impact on making sales easier. It is much closer to measuring the outcome of marketing's efforts instead of just the effort itself.

Sales Wants to Focus on Net New Pipeline and Doesn't Care about "Influenced" Opportunities

Traditionally sales wants to know how many *new* leads are generated by marketing, and this is an important metric to report on. But what about all the leads and opportunities already in the funnel? A marketing touch can help accelerate the sales process. At InsideView, we've come to measure both net new and influenced pipeline for every campaign—and it really gives the most complete picture on the success of a campaign or event.

What Is Sales Afraid Of?

Marketing Is Too Far Removed from the Customer

In our alignment survey, just about half of sales reps say that marketing thinks they know better than sales when it comes to what will work in the field. Sales still sees marketing as just sitting in an office while sales goes out and talks to leads and customers every day. Unfortunately, there is some truth to this, but marketing will never talk to as many customers as sales. What marketing can do is put the customer experience at the forefront of their decision making, and that's where alignment helps. Collaboration opens up more dialogue so both sides can better understand what sales is experiencing, and transparency shows both teams what customers want and how each can contribute to delivering it.

I Don't Have Time to Do My Job and Help Marketing Do Theirs

Alignment isn't about adding work to anyone's plate; it's about focusing on what drives growth. Both teams have to be flexible about time allocation. Maybe they need to change how they do certain things, and maybe they need to take on some new responsibilities, but alignment clarifies what those things are and who is doing them. It also helps sales see what marketing is doing to help make their jobs easier. Salespeople too often run into marketers who are constantly asking, "What should we do to help generate leads?" Sales doesn't know because that's marketing's job! Sales wants recommendations; they'll certainly give input, but they want to know that marketing is bringing their expertise to the table.

Marketing Might Derail My Sales Process

When Tracy first came to InsideView, she discovered sales had asked marketing to stop all communication to opportunities once sales put them in the pipeline. At that point, only sales could communicate with that lead. Sales didn't trust that marketing would communicate the right thing and they were worried that marketing would delay the sales process or drop the ball on a key message. However, sales knew that they couldn't keep that relationship going on their own because the prospect was missing out on key programs that might have been appealing and helped close the deal. The root issue was that marketing did not have the trust of the sales team.

Working together, marketing proved to sales that ongoing touches from marketing to all accounts was a good thing. We focused on helpful, thought-leadership–style content to keep InsideView top-of-mind with the accounts in the working pipeline. That has proven to be an excellent strategy. Initially, when Andrea told her sales team that this was going to happen, there was push back and concern. Marketing paid a lot of attention to the quality and execution of those touches, and sales came to trust and even ask for more support. Most importantly, the response from customers was excellent.

I Just Want My Golf Tournament, Not Those Worthless Event Leads

Sales will frequently point to lead quality as marketing's biggest failure, and this gets us back to data. Alignment opens the data kimono to both teams and everyone can see that last year's marketing event drove $4 million in new business while sales' executive breakfasts only drove $1.5 million. Data from a common source, especially on how it drives pipeline, gives everyone the same perspective from which to collaboratively make decisions.

Marketing Isn't Accountable for Anything that Really Matters

We've already discussed pipeline as an important alignment measure. If you're working toward this goal, marketing will adopt the pipeline measure and will even eventually have compensation tied to pipeline goals. They'll see the financial benefits to themselves and the growth benefits for the business.

Marketing Doesn't Understand the Realities of Being in Sales

The pressure on sales is enormous. A marketer probably won't be fired if they miss their goals one quarter. In sales, that's always a distinct possibility. On the bright side, our alignment survey found that nearly all marketers, 94 percent, agree that sales is a difficult job.

Your company probably has a sales leaderboard; we call ours the *sales ladder*. It's the stacked ranking of every sales rep in your organization and it makes performance a very transparent thing (Figure 2.2). You can see who's doing well and who should be dusting off their resume.

Good sales reps love this type of pressure. They are fed better and bigger leads, they get more time with the company executives, they are invited to more events, and they get to cherry pick the best leads from those events. And they get attention from marketing, because marketing wants to figure out how to replicate their success.

Marketing would *never* want to be ranked this way. There's just too much pressure and, in a marketer's world, there is not a straightforward measure, like revenue, for ranking. Tracy refers to

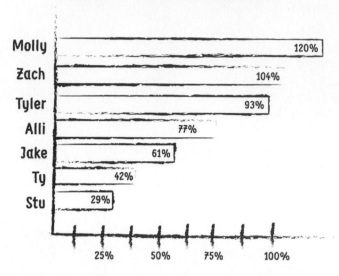

FIGURE 2.2   A typical, stack-ranked sales leaderboard, which leaves no doubt as to which sales reps are performing well and which should be worried about their continuing employment.

this type of pressure as being in the hot seat. Marketers aren't in the hot seat enough to feel and properly react to such pressure.

What will ultimately allay all of these fears on both sides is to bring teams together on pipeline. But to do so, your data needs to be clean and accurate. Your teams need to collaborate on how leads get into the pipeline and what sales needs to close them. Your culture needs to be supportive of healthy tension while still showing respect.

Insights from Leading Both Sales and Marketing

Adrienne Weissman is chief marketing officer and head of sales at G2 Crowd, which provides business software ratings and reviews from real IT and business users. Adrienne is a unique CMO because she runs *both* sales and marketing. That's a huge cultural shift for any B2B company, since it forces sales to report to marketing and it forces marketing to share their leader's focus. While Adrienne initially saw it as a challenge, it has opened her eyes to the power of keeping everyone focused on the revenue prize. It's also shown the need for a culture of flexibility if you're going to be on the cutting edge of sales and marketing alignment.

"It's difficult to find that trust between sales and marketing," Adrienne says. "Leading both has exposed a lot of the challenges between the teams that many companies face. There's a natural friction between sales and marketing and I'm OK with that. Sales is the front end, they take the leads over the finish line, but marketing gets them to that point, so both have obvious contributions to winning revenue."

As Adrienne sees it, the friction comes from not only assigning appropriate credit for the successes, but identifying where challenges happen during an opportunity's path from prospect to closed deal.

"Because they both sit under me, I have a much better handle on what the friction is and how to best align and move in the same direction," she added.

As we've found to be the case for well-aligned teams, the "same direction" is focusing on the end goal. While we advocate pipeline as the metric for marketing, G2 Crowd is striving to measure both sales and marketing on revenue.

"Everyone is responsible for revenue in some way," Adrienne explained. "We even played around with marketing having ownership of a specific portion of revenue recently, but we're not sophisticated as an industry to get to that point yet. When you measure only on deals closed, it's not a true assessment of success. What if we had a full pipeline but we didn't have the right prospects? Or what if the pipeline estimate is great, but we find out later our products don't align to customer needs? Getting closer to a revenue number is the intention."

With such radical ideas, having a culture that supports and encourages flexibility is important. So is being a great leader.

(Continued)

(*Continued*)

"Even within the teams, between individuals, their motivations can be so different," Adrienne continued. "It's a fundamental part of being a leader. You have to figure out what motivates them and know them well enough personally to encourage them at that level."

Running both teams enables Adrienne to see how each member of her team contributes to the overall progress towards revenue, and it's important to recognize their impact.

"It comes down to being a good leader," she concluded. "I want to help them understand the impact they have every day but also provide the vision of where we are going and what their role is in that vision."

Translating Culture into Growth-Driving Behaviors

We are certain that, without growth, customer, and data as key elements of your culture, any alignment initiative will likely fail. But culture is a fuzzy concept. If you ask your teams to collaborate, they may think that simply means copying each other on emails more often. Obviously it's much more than that.

It's sometimes difficult to verbally convey your culture, but it's easy to exhibit the tangible behaviors that you'd like your teams to emulate. With that in mind, here are a few behaviors that we've found to be invaluable as you begin working towards tighter sales and marketing alignment.

Proactively Communicate Well in Advance

As you ramp up your expectations around collaboration, an important component of that will be communication. Teams who haven't worked closely together before will start working together more often and more tightly than they might expect. Encourage them to talk early and talk often. Over-communicating is better, especially at the beginning.

More specifically, give everyone an early warning. Marketing shouldn't blindside sales with a new campaign that they didn't know about. Talk about projects and programs by looking at a four- to six-week calendar in every conversation. Explain what's happening now, what's happening soon, and your strategy for what you'd like to happen eventually.

Be Overly Transparent

Transparency piggybacks on communication. Transparency means several things: providing all of the necessary details, explaining the decision-making process, and reviewing what went into your strategy. While communication gives information, transparency gives the reasoning behind that information.

For example, marketing should share upcoming campaigns with sales, but also share why those targets were chosen, why other channels were not, what the trade-offs were, and why they expect this decision to succeed. Transparency eliminates questions and builds trust.

Transparency also requires a blameless culture. If a mistake is made, the reaction should be to discover the why, not the who.

Make Recommendations; Don't Just Ask Questions

When you're making plans and building your strategy, don't just expect the other side to read your mind and know exactly what you want. Express yourself clearly and be confident in your experience and ideas. Sales knows sales just as marketing knows marketing. Rely on your experience to guide your recommendations.

For example, sales shouldn't ask marketing for more field events. They should be specific about what they want. If they like executive breakfasts in major cities with a key analyst as the featured speaker, they should say so directly. For another upcoming event, marketing may want sales to help with follow-up. In that case marketers should be specific about who should be involved, who the targets are, and what the script will be.

When conveying your plans and goals, be proactive and confident about your decisions. Doing so requires that you've done your homework and have weighed all of the options, and it also requires that you've thought through your decisions.

Get Feedback from Everyone

Marketers may think their new campaign is going to be great, but they shouldn't be overconfident until they get feedback from sales early in the process. Sales will have ideas that marketing might not have considered, and the goal is to work together to find solutions. Soliciting feedback also helps marketing to explain their thinking behind a decision. That gives them an incentive to think things through, and it also gives sales insight into what marketing is doing and how the strategy is being executed.

This doesn't mean that marketing has to take every piece of feedback and incorporate it. They key is to make sales feel heard, find those a-ha moments that the marketing team hadn't considered, and make the whole process better and the end result successful.

Listen First

Sales reps are aggressive and marketers are creative, which leads both to be talkers. Stop talking. Let the other person finish their thought, then ask questions. Get your counterparts to talk about the context of their ideas and actions. Maybe they want to get early feedback on rough ideas, or maybe they want to see how much more the other teams can take on. Whatever the case, don't assume and don't jump in until you understand them.

Tracy has what she calls her "good ideas list." When others are speaking, they frequently have ideas or insights that don't work today, but might be gold in a few weeks or months. Create a mechanism for capturing these ideas and periodically reviewing them. If you aren't listening, you're going to miss some great ideas.

Identify and Work Closely with the Opinion Leaders

In every organization and on every team, people stand out in different areas. Bill may be the expert on the competition while Barb may be the most experienced with deals in a specific industry. They are the opinion leaders. Listen to them. Use them early and often. Take them to lunch. Buy them coffee. Be their best friend.

If you don't know who they are, find out who others trust. Look at the names on the top of the sales ladder. Watch to see who gets the most questions at meetings and how attentive people are to their answers. You'll quickly identify these opinion leaders and, when you say things like, "I talked to Molly who said . . .," you will earn the confidence of your colleagues. On the contrary, if you name-drop Stu, who is always toward the bottom of the sales ladder, those comments will be discounted.

If You Do Nothing Else About Culture, Do These Things

1. Evaluate your cultural readiness for alignment by comparing the favorable culture outlined here with your current company culture. Decide where your culture is hitting the mark and where it needs to change. Develop a concrete list of areas of improvement and potential plans of action.

2. Talk to your CEO about your culture and how it might impact your move toward alignment. Be specific and share your cultural readiness evaluation and your recommended plans of action.

3. Review the pipeline every week with marketing and sales together, and spend enough time to dive into any challenges and areas of success. Look for root causes of both and determine what both marketing and sales can do differently to make improvements. We built a pipeline countdown dashboard showing the number of weeks left in the quarter and the pipeline percentage, broken down by business segment, that we should have reached at each weekly milestone. It lets us see specifically where we need to pay more attention.

4. Capture good ideas from both the sales and marketing teams. You never know where a good idea will come from, even if now is not the time to implement it.

5. Get your tension points out on the table with your executive counterparts. Use communication and transparency to defuse the tension and seek to understand your counterpart's perspectives.

Build Alignment into Every Process

Before we begin, let's repeat our alignment mantra: *Sales can't do it alone and marketing exists to make sales easier.* Now let's consider process and how it affects alignment.

We look at process as a way to define what should be done in most cases, and also as a yardstick to measure the impact of—and determine the reaction to—exceptions. If you don't have a process that everyone in your organization understands and follows, it isn't possible to make exceptions when warranted. As a result, everything becomes an exception and your company runs like the Wild West.

Here's our next bold statement: The old linear sales funnel is dead. Your sales funnel can no longer be depicted as a simple linear path from lead to closed deal. It's now continuous, circular, overlapping. Research by McKinsey & Company found that B2B customers use an average of six different "interaction channels" throughout their decision-making process, and nearly two-thirds of them say they are frustrated by inconsistent experiences.

Since the relationship with the customer is ongoing, customers can engage, pull away, and re-engage when it's convenient for them. All of this adds up to confusion for sales and marketing unless they

47

can adapt to match the buyer. That means more handoffs and touching of leads, which requires better coordination and communication. It also means sales and marketing have to work together to create a strategic plan for engaging with buyers as each buyer takes their unique path.

Process Is Where Your Culture Hits the Road (It's a Bumpy One)

If culture is the map and spirit of the company, process is the highway. Process is where you can make the granular changes to how you interact with your customers to guide them to a sale. It is *hard*. Defining, implementing, and sticking to a process can be tedious. But having a clear one in place should simplify how teams run. And by allowing for exceptions, it enables flexibility while still offering the structure people need to engage in smart analysis and decisions. Be warned, however, that not every person is good at creating and implementing process. In order to succeed, there must be people on your teams who love this style of work, are good at it, and can help everyone else along. Process is at the heart of alignment success, and it needs to be executed correctly.

Creating Your Customer Engagement Strategy

The basis of an aligned process begins with your customer engagement strategy. Alignment takes a shared, customer-centric approach to how sales and marketing interact with each other and with the customer. The company that best responds to the customer's needs will win, and to determine how to do this, sales and marketing have to work together to understand the customer completely. Data openness and integration are critical to having the complete picture.

Customers want simplicity and transparency. They don't want product pitches and marketing fluff; they want knowledge and education that are relevant to their particular situations. They also want to clearly understand how and why your offering's price, features, services, advantages, and other aspects fit their unique business needs.

The challenge for sales and marketing is that the B2B buyer prefers to gather most of this information independently. At worst, sales and marketing have become less integral to the overall buying process. At best, these functions interact with the buyer much later in the cycle. Sales and marketing, together, have to redefine their relationship with the customer. They have to consistently prove their value and do so however the customer wants it. The only way this can happen is for marketing and sales to be in lockstep.

Unfortunately, we've all been caught a bit off guard by the magnitude of misalignment, and we need a back-to-basics movement in order to get back on track. It starts with jointly creating and agreeing on a customer engagement model that fits today's modern buying and selling process.

You probably define your customer journey as a funnel, where marketing finds many prospects to move into the top of the funnel; then marketing and sales work to winnow these down into a number of qualified leads, from which sales takes the promising opportunities and turns them into, hopefully, closed deals. Marketing works the top, sales works the bottom (Figure 3.1).

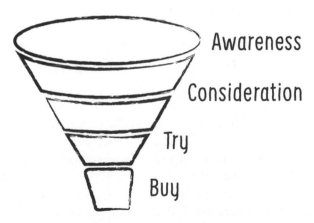

FIGURE 3.1 In the last B2B purchase you were involved with, did you follow the typical linear buying process, shown here, as it was dictated by the vendor? Or did you do your research and take action based on your own needs, processes, and timeline?

This linear customer engagement model is no longer relevant, however, and we're not the only ones seeing it change. Barb Giamanco is a sales, social selling, and social media strategist, and a speaker, advisor, and author who has trained more than 30,000 sales professionals. She's an expert at knowing how sales interacts with buyers, and she's seen big changes in just the past few years.

"Sales and marketing leaders need to wake up," Barb told us recently. "The buyer's behavior is vastly different today than from even just five years ago. They have to stop forcing customers into their *selling* process and start aligning to the customer's *buying* process. And I'm talking from the very first interaction, whether it's sales or marketing. I am very passionate [in my belief] that you never get a second chance to make a first impression."

Sales and marketing must work together to redefine the customer's journey as a continuous cycle with many touchpoints and never-ending opportunities. Marketing doesn't just generate leads and throw them over to sales to close. Marketing nurtures leads until they're ready for sales. Sales is looking for upsell opportunities and relies on marketing to help them grow their footprint with existing customers. It's a constant and continuous journey, and it requires changes to your current sales and marketing processes.

A New Customer Engagement Model for Today's Reality

In our new reality, the old funnel has become a continuous loop of touchpoints and handoffs across the macro phases of find, engage, close, and grow. This model, shown in Figure 3.2, better reflects the realities of today's B2B businesses, where sales and marketing frequently overlap and where fewer businesses treat customers as one-and-done opportunities.

By viewing your customer's journey as a series of continuous engagements and touchpoints, you will have a clear understanding of how both sales and marketing are expected to contribute. You'll also find areas where challenges can occur and where data might be siloed or missing from the process.

Find   **Close**

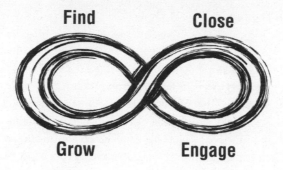

Grow   **Engage**

FIGURE 3.2 The new customer engagement model is continuous, has no distinct beginning or end and it supports customers who move in and out as they please.

A continuous engagement model also magnifies the handoff points, which, as we mentioned earlier, are where problems—particularly with data—usually occur.

Have you ever called your cable company and given all of your account information to the customer service rep, only to be transferred to another rep whose first question is, "Can I get your name and account number?" That's frustrating, right?

When a prospect indicates to marketing that they are interested in your silver service package, you can't blame them for being frustrated when your sales rep's first question is, "What are you interested in?" Prospects expect more, and with the data they've provided, that expectation is fair.

This is just one example of what you're trying to avoid. Sales and marketing alignment will help you to do it. Your first step is redefining your customer engagement model.

Through our conversations with and sales to thousands of companies, we've both found that the find, engage, close, and grow loop is the fundamental basis for the most effective engagement models. The details may change based on your business, but these four main engagement phases exist in every B2B customer relationship. It's simple and easy to understand and, most importantly, it starts the process of alignment.

Its Time Has Come

Andrea has been in sales for years and always used to use a linear funnel. Every sales deck included a chevron design that illustrated the stages of the sales funnel. Marketing handed leads to sales, then sales handed closed deals to a customer care team. Currently at InsideView, in Andrea's sales pipeline review meetings, she talks about classic sales stages for tracking the progress of opportunities. In collaborative sales and marketing meetings, the team uses the continuous buyer journey model, which expands the conversation and covers all aspects of how programs align the teams.

InsideView is a subscription-based company, so the continuous model makes a lot of sense. We want a high level of renewals, so we never consider a deal as won-and-done. It might be a bit more difficult at first to gain support for this model in a traditional company, but when you think about it, almost every business is moving toward a subscription model. Apple wants to sell you an AppleCare warranty plan for your phone. Spotify wants you to subscribe to their overall service instead of buying one song. Even product-based B2B companies sell service plans and offer leasing options because they see the potential of recurring revenue.

The B2B sales process is not linear. You always want to sell more to your customers, expand your footprint, or get introduced to subsidiaries and other groups. You also need to protect your customers from competitors. Think of it as a land-and-expand strategy.

As you're moving to this new model, think about how you really interact with your customers. You'll quickly see that it's not linear and it does not end. If it does, your relationship with your customers might end, too.

Alignment Process Fundamentals

Ask someone on your marketing team to define what makes a lead a lead, and then ask someone on the sales team. In all likelihood, their answers will differ and neither will be completely accurate. The lens each job function looks through will shape the definition of the lead's characteristics and value.

Alignment requires sales and marketing to build trust and understanding at the foundational level, starting by jointly defining the fundamentals. What is a lead? What is a marketing-qualified lead? What is an opportunity?

One initial step toward alignment is to define your lead-scoring model. Before Tracy joined InsideView, Andrea asked how the company defined and scored leads, and the standard response was "because" and "trust us." There was no visibility into the definition, no transparency into the model or the process, and no trust between the teams. Once Tracy came on board as CMO, she dug into our lead-scoring model and found that almost no one knew *how* leads were scored. Once she figured that out, no one could tell her *why* they were scored that way. This was a legacy scoring model that had not grown with the business. We threw it all away and started from scratch, with both of us and our teams involved in defining the new scoring model.

Beyond simple definitions, there is a mishmash of things to keep in mind. Transparency requires that marketing keeps sales in the loop about upcoming campaigns and that sales lets marketing know how leads are performing. It also means that metrics and reports are designed to promote alignment and build pipeline, not point fingers or assign blame.

New roles that straddle sales and marketing, like sales enablement, are also popping up, and these new job functions can help to bridge the gap between teams. Having a solid process eases these new roles into place, setting them up for success, not for headaches.

To keep our team's eyes on the prize, we like to *speak CEO*. That means framing things in terms of your entire business and your customer. We talk about how alignment is strategic for the company, how it's a company-wide initiative, and that the goal is company growth and a better customer experience. This isn't a trivial initiative to have more meetings between sales reps and marketing managers. It's a big deal that improves everyone's chances of success.

By spending time speaking CEO, our teams—at every level— understand the big picture and how they fit. It's more motivating for them, and results come more quickly. Alignment impacts revenue growth and profit margins, brings in more customers, and expands your base and growing market share, so talk about it with that magnitude of importance.

Don't Just Change Processes, Rebuild Them to Support Alignment

Let's now get into the nuts and bolts of alignment. This is where all of your alignment talk turns into action. It's where your teams start to see real day-to-day operational change that indicates progress.

Collaboration and Communication

Working effectively requires you to look beyond the past and toward the future. Remember our saying, "Seek to understand, not to blame." This can be very challenging, but it's the basis of well-aligned teams, and you're really looking for root causes and potential solutions, not for mistakes.

You're also going to be digging into the nitty gritty of your existing processes and metrics and looking deeply into results. In the beginning, it might seem like you're getting bogged down, but open and clear communication helps to keep alignment moving forward, no matter how tedious the work becomes at times.

Collaboration and communication rely on meetings. Not *more* meetings, but *better* meetings. If you think a current meeting is a waste of time, ask yourself why, look at the agenda (if there even is one), and find a way to improve it. Meetings that serve a specific purpose promote both alignment and collaboration, and produce better results.

Meetings are required at both the strategic and tactical levels, and both sales and marketing need to be open to ideas, honest with their feedback, and able to listen to every point of view. Strategic meetings increase awareness of sales and marketing needs and activities, while tactical meetings set specific actions for executing the actual events, campaigns, and launches. Tactical meetings can be conducted efficiently because the stage has been set.

If all of this is starting to sound like a seminar on how to work effectively with people, you're starting to get it. The reality is that most team processes block alignment. Get this fact out in the open now, understand why it's happening and what you need to do, and change it.

Sales + Marketing = Smarketing

At InsideView, we have what we call our Smarketing Meeting every other Friday morning. It's our fun name for a critical review that keeps sales and marketing on the same page. The topics allow us to communicate important details, hold each other accountable, and get input.

Here's our hour-long agenda each week:

- Marketing campaign calendar of what's happening over a rolling six-week period, meaning we cover the past few weeks and the upcoming few weeks. The intent is to review progress on past activities and remove any surprises about future ones.

- Detailed review of the most recently completed campaigns and events and a look at the metrics. This includes a quick discussion of performance against goals and follow-up expectations.

- Update on immediately pending campaigns, with details of what's coming up next week and the week after. Ensure sales is ready for campaign follow-up.

- Bigger picture items. Overview of what's coming up that might impact sales and/or marketing, like a new product launch or a big event that's in the planning stages. Marketing might also preview a creative concept to get feedback from sales.

- Open discussion and brainstorming to cover challenges and process hiccups.

Our Smarketing Meeting has really helped to foster alignment. We've essentially eliminated the phrase "I didn't know that was happening" from both teams. And both sides get weekly feedback on lead performance, which helps marketing decide how to run future campaigns and helps sales give constant feedback on lead quality.

This keeps everyone accountable and aware of needs and changes in perspective.

This meeting has a reputation for being *the place where things happen*. Consequently, we've gotten asked to extend attendance to teams outside sales and marketing, such as the product team. The meeting is also recorded each time, for those who can't make it in person.

Smarketing brings a healthy dose of transparency to campaign performance, follow-up metrics (from sales), pipeline performance, and the cost of campaigns. It is eye opening for sales to know how much a marketing campaign costs the company. And we don't just talk about program dollars; we talk about people time. For instance, as we mentioned earlier, our average webinar takes 40 to 60 hours of marketing muscle to execute. *Muscle* is Tracy's word for marketing resources. It's a great way to refer to your people in a positive way because instead of saying, "We don't have enough resources," she says, "We need more muscle to do that." It goes over much better and helps educate other teams on what energy and time something will take. It has the added benefit of helping marketing not sound like they are whining.

Learning to Share

Remember that alignment doesn't mean that one team is required to get the other team's approval. It means that everyone respects the expertise of their colleagues, listens to their points, and offers their feedback. It's about sharing information, not blocking progress.

There's strategic sharing, where you explain why you're doing what you're doing, and there's performance sharing, where you dig into the ongoing results and learn from them.

Strategic sharing comes into play when marketing discusses campaign strategies and long-term plans with sales reps, and gets early feedback from sales on these plans. It's more than just sharing your marketing calendar. It's about opening up the thought process behind it. If you chose to spend your entire third-quarter event budget on a big trade show instead of five smaller executive breakfast events, explain why, what you're giving up, and what benefits you see.

Strategic sharing also takes place when sales discusses their goals and current performance with marketing. Again, the *why* is more important than the *what*. For example, if sales sets a goal to increase overall sales by 15 percent, discuss why that number was chosen and how they will work with marketing to get there.

In both cases, it is important to explain the thinking behind the decisions and get the other team's input and buy-in before you commit to anything. You can also explain why you decided not to do something, or what you're giving up by taking a particular path. Let the other team see the trade-offs you've had to make and why you made them.

Performance sharing is outlining progress toward goals, pointing out potential misses, and explaining what you're going to do about it. It happens when marketing shares the results of recent campaigns and sales shares the conversion rates from past campaigns.

Tracy and other marketing leaders attend every sales forecast call at InsideView (we call it "revenue sync") simply to stay informed about progress. It's been a great way to get reps to go beyond blaming lead quality for missed goals, and it also puts marketing on the hot seat when leads aren't performing well.

Performance sharing could be as simple as inviting someone from sales to your monthly marketing all-hands meeting or, as we did, inviting someone from marketing to your sales forecast meetings. It could also include sharing dashboards in your CRM and marketing automation systems with each other. Remember that data is at the heart of your performance meetings. If sales and marketing are using different sets of data, it's absolutely not going to work.

Once you begin sharing more information, both teams will be well informed when it's time to roll up your sleeves and make tactical decisions. Knowing that sales productivity is low because a specific campaign's leads are taking longer to convert will help marketing make better campaign and scoring decisions in the future. Knowing that marketing chose to work on fewer campaigns that are highly targeted helps sales change how they approach their first call.

Having both strategic and performance meetings is important. If teams don't understand the strategies behind the performance, the performance meetings will turn into strategy and planning discussions. If you don't understand the results, the strategy meetings will turn into brainstorming sessions.

At this tactical level, you're starting to follow more leads through the entire sales process. For example, both teams will hear the strategy behind a targeted email campaign, then how it performed, how many leads are being qualified, how those leads perform, where they get stuck, where handoffs are missing data, how much pipeline is created, and how much revenue eventually materializes. It becomes incredibly informative and even enlightening for both teams to not only understand the results but also to see how their decisions impact the entire customer life cycle.

Handoffs are an important part of this sharing and, as we discussed before, it's where leads are frequently blocked. When marketing hands a lead to sales, data doesn't always get transferred and reps have to do research themselves. This happens in other types of handoffs too. For example, when sales development hands a lead to outside sales, maybe the asset download history is lost. More sharing allows for faster identification of these handoff problems.

Be the Leader

As change starts to happen, be proactive with your leadership and with getting feedback. Talk to your team and the other team frequently and at all levels. Ask questions. Get them to open up one on one and in groups. Prove to them that they can talk about bad news or challenges without assigning blaming. We'll talk more about this leadership role in Chapter 4.

Jointly Define Everything

At this point, you may be thinking that your lead-scoring model works well or that everyone understands what has to occur to change a lead to an opportunity. That's great, but are you positive that everyone knows and understands *why*?

Defining your process and metrics again promotes transparency. Doing it together builds ownership, trust, and collaboration.

Even if you think you know the answer, ask yourself what makes a lead a marketing-qualified lead. What data is used? Where does it come from? What if it's missing? Is that a good measure of lead qualification? What are the conversion rates across different stages of the sales cycle?

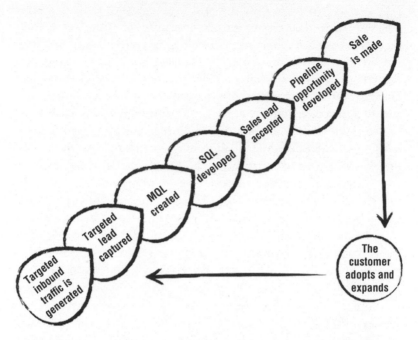

FIGURE 3.3 Forrester Research advises companies to use a lead-to-customer chain to focus on key outcomes. It provides a great framework for defining everything from a target to an opportunity.

Source: Forrester Research, Inc., "Build An Adaptive, Efficient Process To Elevate Leads To Revenue," March, 2016

In the March 2016 report "Build An Adaptive, Efficient Process To Elevate Leads To Revenue," Forrester Research's B2B marketing analyst, Lori Wizdo, offers up a lead-to-customer results chain with detailed definitions, which can be your guide to starting your own definition process (Figure 3.3).

For example, she defines a marketing-qualified lead as "a lead for which sufficient data has been captured to determine if it looks enough like the ideal target prospect so that communication, qualification, and engagement would be cost effective." That's the level of detail you should strive for. Sales and marketing should work together to further define what is "sufficient data" to enable whatever communication (again, define it—is it emails, phone calls, etc.?), qualification, and engagement is desired.

We've worked with a lot of companies who use lead-scoring models that are just too simple. If a lead opens an email and visits your website, that doesn't mean much these days, but in many companies that triggers a call from a sales rep. There are no other qualifications, like industry or company size or prior activity. Worse yet, no one ever analyzed the correlation between lead attributes and conversion rates to determine what is important. That just seems like a productivity killer, especially when you probably have (or can buy) most of the data that's missing to make even better lead qualification decisions.

Lead scoring is just one example of where you can begin to jointly define and redefine what's important. Define—and write down—what turns a prospect into a lead, the base information required in contact and account records, what makes an opportunity, what makes a sales-qualified lead, and so on. Also look at how you dispose of qualified leads. Do they go back to marketing or are they disqualified?

Again, it might seem remedial to do this—everyone knows what a lead is—but don't be too sure. You need to start over from this basic level. Even if things are working well, take this opportunity to write down why and be sure everyone understands it.

Create SLAs for Both Teams

Service-level agreements (SLAs) are great tools to help you set and agree on expectations across both teams. It eliminates arguments later on, and you'll always have these to point to down the road. Remember that sales and marketing should always have some level of healthy tension between them. Creating reasonable SLAs will help maintain that tension.

These SLAs don't have to be long, formal documents. They are simply agreements on performance. For example, they could set the number of qualified leads to be delivered by marketing each quarter or the expected level of data present in a contact record before sales is expected to take on a lead. A sales SLA can include the time allowed for a rep to follow up on new leads or the information required when a lead is disqualified.

At InsideView, we expect sales to accept or reject newly qualified marketing leads within two days, and then to follow up on leads within another two days. We agreed on that together with input from our frontline sales reps. Although we think it's aggressive, we know it's achievable given the size and experience of our sales team.

As we discussed this specific SLA, the eyes of many of our marketers were opened just by understanding the process sales goes through to consume, evaluate, and qualify leads. Some thought sales just sees a new lead and calls them. They didn't understand that reps scour our CRM for related leads, research company news, mutual connections, and much, much more.

On the flip side, marketing can't just keep dumping leads on sales and expect sales to live up to their SLA. One marketing SLA at InsideView gives sales a six-week notice on new campaigns and reminds them every week until the campaign hits. That happens in our Smarketing Meeting, where we deliver a rolling six-week campaign review each week.

We also know when to back off of these SLAs. We ran two very successful webinars recently, each pulling in around 2,000 leads. Obviously, that eventually created a backlog of leads sales had to plow through, and it took a lot longer than two days. The same backlog happens after large events. In both cases, even the marketing SLA changes a bit, and we flag leads as "super-hot" to show they should be given priority. That's not something we typically do, but we do it to help manage the backlog and the process changes based on the specifics of the campaign or event. SLAs help you hold your counterpart's feet to the proverbial fire, but it's important to be realistic when conditions change. This is another example of having a defined process but allowing for exceptions when needed.

Another concept we've developed as a direct result of our alignment on SLAs is what we call "real-time marketing." This happens primarily at events, where we snap a photo of a hot lead's business card with our phone and send it to the responsible sales rep. It results in a real-time follow-up with the lead, and it makes an impression. Whereas most marketing follow-up happens after the event, we're aligned and focused on hot leads in the moment. No, it's definitely not scalable. But it gets us engaged well before the noise of the event follow-up from dozens or hundreds of marketing departments who start their follow-up campaigns a few days later.

Who Are We Selling to Anyway?

Some companies go to great lengths to define their perfect customers with detailed customer personas. We've seen marketing documents from big B2C (business-to-consumer) brands that contain chapters on individual customer personas, with detailed profiles and even names, like "Bodhi, a single, twentysomething professional who enjoys extreme outdoor activities, drives a hatchback to hold his gear, and puts a premium on buying products that showcase his adventure-seeking nature."

In the B2B world, personas seem to be just hitting their stride. We're seeing more marketing teams creating personas that sketch out the types of buyers they are targeting. These cover titles, market trends, objectives, challenges, and pain points. Personas may even drill into value statements, typical org chart positioning, and budget sizes (Figure 3.4).

PERSONA:	Director of Marketing
REPORTS TO:	CMO or VP of Marketing
RESPONSIBILITIES:	Executes marketing strategy, prioritizes campaigns, ensures lead quality
PRIORITIES:	Generating quality leads, managing campaign teams
KEY METRICS:	Lead-to-close rates, win rates, campaign ROI

FIGURE 3.4 A sample buyer persona in summary form, which states the key characteristics of a target, what's important to them, and how they are measured, to help both sales and marketing determine how to best engage.

What these personas do is define your ideal prospect. Generally, they're created by marketing and then leveraged by sales. That's a mistake. Collaboration creates joint ownership and opens discussions around target markets, ideal levels and titles, and market and competitive trends that should impact targeting.

If your organization is like most companies, a discussion of target market is long overdue. Marketing usually sets the target markets based on research, such as market size, number of potential customers, competitive pressure, and so on. But sales hears directly from customers so they have more data on pain points, budgets, and the market's true situation.

Sales is also making the calls and talking to leads; they are the ones on the front lines of the business. They will have to deliver the message marketing eventually creates, so getting their participation and buy-in early helps identify gaps in training or the need for marketing to develop industry-specific content or persona-specific campaigns. They also already have the pulse of the market, and will have a good perspective on what will work and what will not.

Where to Begin with Process Alignment

We've mentioned lead scoring a few times and that's always a great place to start. It's a handoff point between sales and marketing and it's frequently a friction point as well. As you drill into your scoring model and process, you will want to look upstream to determine if things like lead source or other attributes should be considered. For example, should an event lead be scored on a different model than a webinar lead? Should a manufacturing lead be scored differently than a finance lead? These conversations matter and they could point you toward other areas that need to be jointly defined.

Metrics and measurements are also a great place to begin. Sales and marketing must be aligned on what's being measured, how it's being measured, and why it matters. It helps to set expectations for performance evaluations, which uncovers differences in data that might lead to disagreements or divergent decisions down the road.

How you choose to start building an aligned set of metrics is unique to you, but consider the following suggestions. Remember that both sales and marketing contribute to all of these points, so this list includes important performance metrics for both teams. Andrea refers to these as the *attributes of sales velocity*.

- **Number of opportunities** in a given period. Leveraging your ideal customer profile and tapping into a solid business problem will give the teams repeatability and can generate momentum. This is measured by the number of deals a rep can close each month, which also indicates how many deals each rep can handle in parallel. If deals require a lot of hand-holding, reps may only be able to take on a few at a time. If marketing provides the right tools to push leads along, sales can handle more.

- **Average deal value** will guide you on how many deals need to close to reach the revenue goals. In turn, by using conversion rates, marketing knows how many leads they need to produce. If average deal size is changing, it can be an early warning signal that something very good or very bad is happening.

- **Win rates** have many factors, which are sometimes a reflection of sales effectiveness and other times a reflection of the quality of the pipeline. Creating a baseline win rate and measuring the changes over time will provide signals of the lead scoring model, quality of leads, and effectiveness of the sales teams. Win rates also tell you the amount of pipeline needed. The ideal is typically a 3x coverage model, meaning you win 33 percent of your deals, but it varies by industry.

- **Sales cycle length** shows how many days it takes to close a qualified lead. This impacts SLAs between sales and marketing, but it also reflects the effectiveness of your sales team, your lead-scoring model, and the quality of your leads. If cycles are slow, maybe leads aren't quite qualified or marketing isn't providing the right content, or maybe sales needs better training. If they are moving fast, you will want more of those types because you've hit gold.

Pulling all of these measurements together gives the formula for sales velocity, which is a measure of how many dollars in revenue each

$$\text{Sales Velocity} = \frac{\left(\begin{smallmatrix}\text{\# of}\\\text{Opportunities}\end{smallmatrix}\right) \times \left(\begin{smallmatrix}\text{Avg Deal}\\\$\$\$\end{smallmatrix}\right) \times \left(\begin{smallmatrix}\%\\\text{Win Rate}\end{smallmatrix}\right)}{\text{Length of Sales Cycle}}$$

FIGURE 3.5 Calculating your sales velocity forces sales to dig deeper into sales metrics and forces marketing to better understand where they can contribute to sales effectiveness and, therefore, growth.

rep is bringing in per day (Figure 3.5). Since a quarter has a specific number of days, sales velocity will tell you how you're tracking toward your overall goals.

If your sales velocity isn't enough to hit your targets, you can either increase the numerator or decrease the denominator. Both sales and marketing have shared responsibility across every metric in this calculation.

Do It Right: Use Content as a Catalyst for Alignment

Robert Wahbe is the co-founder and CEO at Highspot, which develops sales engagement software. He works with companies of all sizes to bring their content under control and make it easily accessible, as he's seen content be a great point to kick off discussions around sales and marketing alignment.

"Content is a big issue for companies, and it causes issues between sales and marketing in companies of all sizes," Robert explains. "In a large organization, say with 10,000 people, they may have 4,000 or 5,000 pieces of content. When you get to a huge enterprise, say 100,000 people, they might have 10 times that volume of content. That's active content, covering complex product lines, in different languages, for different regions.

(Continued)

(*Continued*)

It's a huge undertaking because marketing created the content but sales needs to be able to find it and use it. So do you organize it by product line, which is how marketing thinks, or by sales stage, which is how sales thinks? It's the first step in bringing those two teams together."

Having these deep and complex conversations about content opens the door to more and deeper conversations around your buyer's journey, your offerings, and how to grow your business.

"It gets companies talking about geographies, products, the buyer's journey, and the seller's journey, and it's all difficult," Robert says. "What we start to see at this point is sales tends to sell by bundles or offers, not by individual products. Marketing creates content by products, not by bundles. Then sales starts talking about the mechanics of a deal, the mechanical sales stages in their CRM system. That's how sales sees the customer interaction, but marketing never sees it that way."

Robert has watched as, time and again, just talking about content gets marketing and sales talking about more strategic and business-altering topics. Starting with content management almost tricks them into the need for tighter alignment, from simple definitions to which markets to target.

"The questions they start to ask are hard," Robert says. "So sales and marketing need to agree on a common language to think about content, which turns into a common language to think about their business. Content is just the foot in the door to these bigger conversations."

"Next they'll begin to analyze what's happening with their content," adds Robert. "They'll see what's being used, how, and by who and when. Most quickly find out much of their content is never touched. It either can't be found, doesn't meet the needs of sales or the customer, or doesn't match the customer's use case. That sparks other discussions about what content is even needed."

"Eventually, they get talking about how content drives revenue. Is this content changing our business? Is it increasing sales velocity? Is it speeding up our deal cycles? Now they have the data, so sales stops yelling about content and is happier and marketing can back up what they're doing and how their content is creating a return on investment."

Although Robert sees marketing more as the driver of alignment and content management, it's both sales and marketing who ultimately benefit.

"It doesn't matter who drives the look at content," Robert concludes. "It always leads to conversations about how to grow the business, and it always drives better sales and marketing alignment."

Keep an Eye Out for Trouble

If leads start going off track or an opportunity is stalling, don't forget to look at metrics that serve as early warning indicators. This is going to be different and a challenge for every company, and it takes a joint effort to determine what signals a warning. Investigating this also shines light on the quality and accuracy of your data, the effectiveness of your handoffs and conversions, and the level of communication established.

Look at one aspect of a sale cycle to determine the impact on win rates. The number of meetings before a product demonstration, for example, might correlate with win rates. If win rates are low when a demonstration isn't conducted in the first three meetings, then maybe demonstrations should be pushed earlier or not at all. Don't immediately point the finger at demonstrations, in this case. Maybe your process puts them too early or too late. Maybe leads should be further qualified before a demonstration. Maybe other steps should be added before or after.

InsideView's CRO, John Kelly, has a dashboard of early warning indicators he splits into leading and lagging indicators. It helps him identify potential issues early so he and his team have time to correct them before it's too late (Figure 3.6).

Early warning indicators signal a deal is off track, engagement efforts need work, or miscommunication or fumbled handoffs are

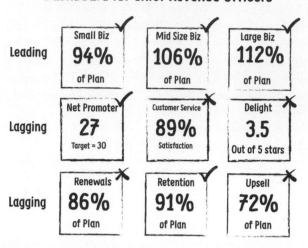

Dashboard for Chief Revenue Officers

	Small Biz	Mid Size Biz	Large Biz
Leading	94% of Plan	106% of Plan	112% of Plan

	Net Promoter	Customer Service	Delight
Lagging	27 Target = 30	89% Satisfaction	3.5 Out of 5 stars

	Renewals	Retention	Upsell
Lagging	86% of Plan	91% of Plan	72% of Plan

FIGURE 3.6 By tracking and constantly reviewing both leading (before the win) and lagging (after the win) indicators of success, you can identify potential issues while there's still time to fix them.

causing pain. Sales and marketing are usually both responsible for fixing the issue.

Always Be Brainstorming

At the CMO and VP levels, you need to frequently discuss what-if scenarios and how they would impact your strategies. What if you land that big customer? What if a new competitor targets your market? What if that great sales rep resigns? What if we get 25 percent more marketing budget next year? What if we hired one more great sales rep? What if the CEO decides to expand into Europe this year instead of next year?

The two of us make it a point to have dinner regularly and talk at a high level. We often talk about things we want to do next year or the year after. We talk about those early warning indicators bubbling up that we don't need to address today but, if we do nothing, they'll be a real problem next year.

Our CEO likes to ask us periodically what we would do right now if we had an additional $100,000. When we're always brainstorming good ideas, the great ideas recur again and again. When he asks us this question, we can offer an idea immediately and know it's already been vetted at a high level. We also keep a good-idea folder. When we have a bright idea that we can't do today, we jot it down and keep a running list. When an opportunity comes up, we might go back and pull that idea off of the shelf.

Use Alignment-Positive Metrics

We've mentioned metrics a lot in this chapter. They are obviously important to everyone at every level, but let's reiterate that pipeline is the most alignment-positive metric you have. It's the best metric to rally around and it requires tight alignment to really make it grow.

If you're ready, look at both sourced pipeline and influenced pipeline. Sourced pipeline is a net new opportunity that has entered your cycle. Influenced pipeline are deals already in the pipeline that marketing continues to influence. It helps you see where marketing can impact cycle times and deal sizes throughout the process.

In sales, we look at four key metrics: number of deals currently in the pipeline, win rates, average selling price, and cycle length. Those are three quality metrics and one quantity metric—and that's by design. Marketing used to be measured just on the top of the funnel: number of leads. Now, by looking at the *quality* of the leads in the pipeline and how often they convert into revenue, marketing sees the impact of their work.

Our marketing team also measures its impact on awareness, using the share-of-voice metric. We want to show sales that marketing efforts in PR, advertising, social campaigns, and more are providing air cover for them. We have selected four key competitors and show the share-of-voice measure each quarter, with a stated goal of always being in the first position.

Remember to share these metrics constantly. Let marketing see what sales has to work with and how some leads are harder to close or less valuable than others. Let sales see marketing is making adjustments that can help them make more money. It fosters cooperation and supports the overall value of alignment.

Do It Right: Use Social Selling as a Catalyst for Alignment

Grad Conn is the CMO for Microsoft's U.S. commercial business. He's also a strong proponent of social selling, and has seen firsthand how social selling techniques have allowed sales teams to outperform those who don't use them. Success, however, requires a tight relationship between sales and marketing.

"To be a good social seller, it's not about sending emails," Grad explains. "You have to be posting and talking about your industry, becoming a subject matter expert. That content has to come from marketing because a sales rep's time is so precious. Social selling is a great way of linking sales and marketing. Marketing has the content sales wants to post, which is forcing the sales-marketing partnership to become stronger."

We've all seen the numbers on how much of the sales cycle is completed before a sales rep is ever consulted. Grad points to those findings as more proof of the need for social selling.

"If you're not part of the conversation early and you're not part of that social journey, you're not going to be a part of the final decision," Grad says.

Grad breaks social selling down into four phases: discover, prospect, influence, and engage. Using that methodology, Grad and his teams have been able to make many more connections with potential buyers. They've even seen an increase of more than 40 percent in reps' online profiles being viewed by key decision makers. That means their social selling overtures are being seen and acted upon by their targets. What they also found was that more than 80 percent of the leads being engaged with were outside of IT and with business unit decision makers. These results are very encouraging.

"The social sellers are driving revenue," Grad added. "We're seeing 42 percent more opportunities among social sellers and a 116 percent increase—more than doubling—their pipeline. Looking across the U.S., we've seen a direct correlation between the rate of adoption of social selling within a district and the success of that district in terms of hitting quota."

With marketing's help, sales sees more success. When things work, teams become more aligned in more areas, but it can begin with something as (relatively) simple as social selling.

If You Do Nothing Else About Process, Do These Things

As you read this list, it may all seem too much in the weeds or too tactical. It's not—these are things you need to do. We're assuming here that you've defined your ideal customer profile and both sales and marketing were involved and support it.

1. Schedule a weekly or biweekly sales and marketing meeting. Call it the Smarketing Meeting or Alignment-Generator Meeting or something that forces the teams to remember it and know what it's for.

2. Dig into your lead-scoring model, really understand it and why it's designed that way, document it, and share it with both sales and marketing.

3. Define a lead, a marketing-qualified lead, and an opportunity, then write them down and share them among the teams.

4. Start reviewing pipeline in your weekly marketing meetings. Get someone from sales in to define the terms used, explain why different metrics are important, and point to where sales is feeling pain and seeing success.

5. Create an SLA that identifies the minimum contact and company data required before marketing can pass a lead to sales as well as the lead follow-up time expected from sales for typical leads.

6. Conduct a hot-seat preparation meeting at least a day before your next big sales and marketing meeting. It's easy to do, just have the marketing person present to you and pepper them with questions.

Chapter 4

An Aligned Organization Requires a Different Kind of Leader

Remember our mantra: *Sales can't do it alone and marketing exists to make sales easier.* Also remember that, as the leaders of the frontline teams, alone you have a lot of power, but together you can both be better and more successful.

As we've said before, it's pretty clear business is rapidly changing, both from the outside in and the inside out. We are experiencing every day the new realities of dealing with better-informed, savvier, and better-connected customers and competitors. But, you're also dealing with the changing demands and requirements of your own role as a sales or marketing leader.

To be successful, we need to have increasingly broad and advanced skills, but more importantly, we need to have vision beyond our own domains. CMOs and sales VPs must understand how data and information flow through systems, how technologies can be used to impact success, and what the complete customer life cycle from onboarding to support to renewals looks like.

Take YouTube as an example of a new technology that has impacted B2B. It's barely 10 years old and when it first launched, no one ever thought a site filled with funny, grainy, shaky videos of kids and cats would morph into a critical tool for B2B marketers. Fast-forward to today and you'll find more than 1,000 videos on Oracle's YouTube channel. Accenture's videos have been viewed one million times; Siemens' channel has nearly 50,000 subscribers and more than 6,000 videos. Browser search results pages show advertisements for IT infrastructure companies and white paper downloads. Searching for "kids and cats" still returns more than 8 million videos, but it's not just a domain of entertainment anymore.

The point is that the rapidly changing world requires adaptable sales and marketing leaders. Furthermore, it requires even tighter collaboration and alignment. Marketing needs the frontline insights from sales to recognize the changes and sales needs the broad product and market knowledge from marketing to better articulate their messages and fight competition. The need for alignment is obvious and it's required. It is impossible to do either function optimally without support from the other, and this change starts at the top.

Is Alignment Obvious or Is It a Stretch Goal?

Unfortunately, alignment doesn't happen on its own. The sales and marketing leaders must drive it, regardless of whether they are selling the idea to the CEO or if the CEO has mandated it.

Jay Fulcher is a noted entrepreneur. He is the former CEO of both Ooyala and Agile Software and has been a sales executive at some of the largest enterprise software companies. He's also one of Andrea's key career mentors. Fulcher doesn't see alignment as an issue because he not only expects it to happen, he hires sales and marketing leaders with the vision to see beyond alignment's benefits.

"Misalignment isn't a problem in my world," Jay explains. "In the past twelve years, as CEO of two companies, it was never an issue with my CMOs and VPs of sales. Their roles have morphed. Sales executives are thinking more like CMOs and strong CMOs spend lots of time in the field and lots of time figuring out how to sell.

"A good leader today can't run sales or marketing unless they've been in the shoes of the other organization. The most recent senior people I hired to lead marketing have had sales experience. They had specifically taken roles in sales to boost their marketing careers. They could speak the language and talk to the issues that sales brings up. On the sales side, the best executives I've worked with are those that have spent time immersing themselves in marketing, understanding the models, and understanding funnel development.

"I just haven't seen huge issues around the need to push sales and marketing towards alignment," he concluded.

Jay is on one end of the spectrum, ahead of the curve on alignment, and he expects his executives to be as well. On the other end of the spectrum, some companies are so misaligned they require heavy lifting before they can even begin the process of alignment. Leadership needs to be prepared and the current effectiveness and abilities of your sales, marketing, and adjacent teams needs to be truthfully evaluated. Are your reps self-sufficient or do they need packaged, easy-to-sell offers? Does marketing supply rigid messaging and expect sales to make deals happen within limited parameters? Is there a lot of turnover in the teams or the leadership?

It's these types of questions that help you understand your starting point. It's not just a question of collaboration on how sales operates. Marketing needs to understand their challenges as well. Are they willing to take accountability across the entire pipeline? Are they able to work with sales to develop, tweak, and improve the messaging? Does marketing engage with customers after deals are won?

For some organizations where alignment seems like a far-off nirvana, you'll have some soul searching to do before you start down the path. That doesn't mean you shouldn't be prepared to try, however.

Attributes of an Aligned Leader

Alignment forces sales and marketing to work closely together. If you work well within the traditional territorial and adversarial sales-marketing relationship, then you're in store for a shocking adjustment. But if you're a natural collaborator who approaches a disagreement as a chance to sell the other team on your ideas or convince them to support your strategies, then you're well positioned. Beyond your outlook, you'll need a few more basic skills.

Collaborative

Recognizing that you can't do it alone helps you be more open and engaging. But also trust that the other person is listening and will ask questions if they need to. Collaboration is a two-way street. Do your part and expect them to do theirs.

Listen to your customers, too. You cannot rely on staff to tell you what's happening in the market. You have to be out in the world, not only listening, but telling everyone why your offering is the greatest thing in the world. Sales VPs are naturally going to be involved with deals, listening to prospects, and hearing customers. Marketing needs to get involved at similar levels.

Transparent

Openness and transparency are more critical than ever before. If you're building an organization that's aligned around growth and customer, raising issues won't be seen as finger pointing.

Don't assume that people are judging you for putting the problem out there, even if it's your problem alone. You don't need to have all of the answers, but you need to be comfortable enough to expose your decisions to scrutiny. Make a statement and get people to rally around it. It's frustrating when no one in a meeting discusses the elephant in the room. Meetings give you a forum to bring up concerns and you should take full advantage of that.

Transparency works both ways. When someone else is being transparent, they are trusting you to provide feedback and assistance. They are asking for help, so help them. Also, don't give people the opportunity to disappoint you. If the elephant is in their corner, bring it out. Allow for the opportunity to open up the dialog. Make it easy for those less apt to bring up the harder topics. You're trying to help them facilitate change—and you're the leader.

Analytical

Data is constantly being collected and must be effectively analyzed. Looking at your marketing automation and CRM dashboards every Monday morning isn't enough. You must have the ability to understand the importance of all of the data being collected, where it's coming from, if it's clean and accurate, how it's connected to other data and systems, and, finally, what it's saying. This is more than a basic knowledge of your CRM system; it's a deeper understanding of all of your systems, what they are capable of, and how data flows through and between them.

Being able to interpret the data is just as important. A knowledge of statistics and statistical methods should be in your skillset to help you discern what's important and what's not. You should understand if different indicators correlate and be able to recognize the difference between a trend and an anomaly. But, being realistic, you're an executive, not a data scientist. You should be able to talk about what the data means and what it says about your business in a way that goes well beyond click-through rates and pipeline forecasts. You're not expected to do the data analysis, but you are expected to ask the right questions. If you don't understand statistics and A/B testing, you'll make wrong decisions.

It also takes a bit of gut to temper what the data tells you. Kelly Steckelberg is the CEO at Zoosk, an online dating company and she likes to say, "If you torture data long enough, you'll get to the answer you want." In other words, use your head and don't blindly follow your dashboards.

"I believe in mixing data with a healthy sense of intuition," Kelly says. "I want data to substantiate a decision, but at a certain point, you are the person who has to make the call. With big data and business intelligence everywhere, you're pressured to follow the data. But step back and think, use your intuition to decide how to move forward, and use the data to inform your decision."

Tech-Savvy

Both sales and marketing are tech-driven, marketing admittedly more so. But with so much reliance on marketing automation and CRM systems, you can't rely on others to simply tell you what's happening.

You should have the skills and smarts to dig into your systems, run the reports you want, dig into the opportunities you're interested in, and understand how your web analytics data contributes to your lead-scoring model.

Beyond those systems, the explosion of smaller, more targeted tech, such as SEO tools, social media managers, predictive sales tools, and others, forces you to have an understanding of sales and marketing technology in general. As you grow, as markets change, as new priorities arise, you'll likely be involved in selecting a couple of pieces of significant technology every year. When the talk turns to integration, APIs, workflows, the cloud, and analytics, you'll want to be able to envision what these tools can do for you and understand how they can help.

Customer-Focused

We've made it clear that the customer must be a rallying point. It's worth repeating here because being customer focused is an easy characteristic to cultivate if you're not already a believer. What it takes is empathy. There's a constant need to be in tune with your customers and how they are feeling. As the leader, you can't rely on your staff to interface with customers and pass along their feedback. This is a hands-on skill, and you need to gather firsthand feedback.

Beyond empathy, it takes work and travel, thick skin, and an open ear. Happy customers are wonderful, but unhappy customers are much more useful. Understanding when to listen genuinely is critical. Knowing what to do with what you heard is even more critical.

Inspire Your Team

When your team is down, when quotas are missed or campaigns go south, it's the leader's role to look at all of the great stuff they've done. We don't want to minimize this role by making it seem like a cheerleader, but that's essentially what this is. You have to be a constant source of positivity about alignment. You can be transparent and share your concerns or point out challenges, but you're in charge of overcoming those challenges or inspiring your team to overcome them.

You're also the primary role model. What you do, how you act, what you say is all consumed by your team. Commit yourself to alignment success and prove it in your actions.

Choose (and Hire) the Right Team

We got lucky at InsideView. When Tracy came in as CMO, Andrea was eager for a counterpart who wanted to drive alignment with her. We got along great from the very first meeting during the interview process. We're also great friends now, which we owe to our successful working relationship and our genuine respect for each other.

For you, it may not be so easy. When we talk with others in our leadership roles, we hear the common refrains from CMOs ("My sales VP is a bully") and from sales VPs ("My CMO just doesn't listen"). That's a fact in most companies, and it's one of the reasons why misalignment has become such a widespread problem.

While you can't choose your counterpart (although you most likely have a say in who will be next or how long the current person stays), it is important to build your own team into one that understands and supports the need for sales and marketing alignment. That means hiring for the traits we've outlined in this chapter: analytical, tech savvy, eager for collaboration, willing to step into the shoes of their counterparts, and so on.

It's hard to ensure the right selection simply by asking questions in an interview. One way to increase your chances of getting a great fit with every hire is using your own network to find candidates. Sebastian Grady, the president at Rimini Street, an independent provider of enterprise software support for Oracle and SAP, recently told us how they ensure new sales hires are well suited to their culture of alignment.

"Our head of sales personally vets and hires everyone in sales," Sebastian says. "He does a lot of back-channel checks and most of our hires come only via connections. Occasionally, mistakes might be made and we get a new hire who just doesn't work out. When that happens, the candidates are most likely from outside of our network."

Alignment's Impact on Recruiting

Nancy Malkin has more than 20 years of experience running Curphey & Malkin Associates, a talent recruitment agency focused on technology companies. In total, Nancy has been in the recruiting business for over 30 years so she's seen wave after wave of trends in corporate initiatives and the hottest must-have skills. Recently, however, Nancy has seen a significant and lasting change in how sales and marketing executives are recruited to fulfill their evolving roles and she answered our questions about recruiting with an eye on alignment.

Is Alignment Entering the Hiring Process?

"The movement toward more aligned sales and marketing teams is happening very quickly, even in the hiring process. I'm seeing more marketing candidates being interviewed by members of the sales team. That's a great move, because marketing has to work with sales quite a bit. Sales has a much stronger say in who marketing hires, and that helps with alignment.

"I'm also seeing misalignment being mentioned more often as a reason for leaving a company. Sales and marketing professionals want to be successful. They want to build their resumes. So when the teams aren't getting along, that limits their success. When sales isn't getting what they need from marketing to win deals, they leave. When marketing isn't appreciated or valued by sales, they leave.

"Sales VPs are also getting more onboard with alignment. They are realizing the value of marketing, and that's becoming more of a topic in interviews for sales executives."

How Have Sales and Marketing Leaders Changed?

"I'm seeing more turnover in the executive ranks these days. It used to be that sales VPs would stick around for a minimum of three years, but now they are changing jobs much more rapidly, as much as every year. There's also more of a generational difference. Younger workers don't seem to have an issue with changing companies after a year if they aren't happy, while older hiring managers won't look at a resume if a person hops every 18 months.

"On the marketing side, the CMO role is much different today. In some companies they run product management and inside sales; in other companies, those roles aren't on their team. It keeps shifting, however."

What Is Changing Within the Marketing Team?

"One aspect driving marketing is obviously the Internet. Having SEO experience a decade ago was unheard of. Now, not only do CMOs need that, they need demand-generation experience, branding expertise, communications expertise—and CEOs want every candidate to have it all. It's very hard to find, and given that it's a candidate's market, especially in tech, salaries have jumped so CEOs want the perfect person.

"Related to technology, I'm starting to see people hiring for the role of VP of digital marketing, someone who runs the entire digital marketing team. It shows the increasing importance of the digital realm within the marketing team, and it shows the level at which CMOs need to understand the digital realm.

"From the sales perspective, reps need content so they love content creators. Lots of companies are hiring dedicated content creators in marketing, so CMOs have to be knowledgeable at that level."

What Is Changing Within the Sales Team?

"There's been a lot of specialization within the sales team. There's a big difference between the hunters and the farmers, and that's been split across lead qualification and inside sales and outside sales. The demand is for sales specialists, not just a sales rep.

(Continued)

> (*Continued*)
>
> "The buyer today is also more powerful and wants to be engaged by a knowledgeable and proficient sales rep. It's to the point that industry experience is more important than sales experience when sales is hiring. Sales VPs want to hire reps that have experience in their market and other experience is secondary."

Be Cool under Pressure

When you begin pushing for alignment, you're stepping into the spotlight. Whether you're with executive peers or with your own team, exploding or losing your cool undermines your trust. While this might seem like Leadership 101 stuff, it's important to reiterate here because alignment will force you to wade into sensitive areas where you will uncover all kinds of problems. Meetings will get tense, especially in the early days of the alignment process.

We both have stories about raising our voices in meetings or having voices raised at us and we're sure everyone has experience with these incidents. Sometimes a point has to be made strongly. Going beyond that raised voice is where you begin to lose respect from others. Knowing your own hot buttons and your own warning signs of stress—heart racing, fist clenching, whatever—will help you defuse yourself and the situation. We've both found that a simple statement like "Let's take this offline and discuss it later" can work wonders.

Be Willing to Listen and Learn

Andrea likes to point out the psychology behind this aspect of leadership. It becomes less about your company and alignment and more about people and interpersonal skills. Salespeople are smart enough to know that they aren't great marketers. They're also smart enough to know a healthy relationship requires listening, asking questions for clarity, and being able to take feedback that you might not want to hear. The listening part is key. Sometimes, just talking about a topic and letting it be heard is enough.

Once a thorny issue is out there, Andrea recommends letting the other person digest what they just heard. Let them ask you clarifying questions or offer to talk at another time in detail or one on one. You want to prevent your comments from being misinterpreted as blame or as being part of a bigger issue than it really is, but you also want to be sure that early warning signs are detected and understood.

Ultimately, sometimes people just need to get things off of their chest. Our Smarketing Meeting at InsideView is a perfect opportunity for teams to raise issues in a forum specifically designed for that purpose. We made this clear when we started the meeting and it's worked out better than expected. Everyone knows that we're there to talk without pointing fingers, and that really encourages people to open up. It also provides a time for us to follow up on past discussions or give updates on progress or roadblocks until an issue is closed out.

Do It Right: Follow These 10 Points to Improve Your Leadership Skills

Heidi Bullock is Marketo's vice president of demand generation. She's also been a competitive soccer player since she was five years old. Being part of a sports team has done more to inform Heidi's leadership style than any professional role has. Her approach is rooted in making others the heroes and it leans heavily on inspiration and support instead of telling people what to do.

Through her years as both a competitive soccer player and a marketing leader, Heidi has developed a set of tips for guiding leaders. We're sharing them with you not only to improve your ability to align, but also to improve your skills as a leader in general.

Here are Heidi's 10 considerations for leaders and aspiring leaders:

1. You are a coach to your department and a player among your peer group/team.
2. A simple and sincere thank you goes a long, long way.
3. Dare to actually care about people.

(Continued)

(*Continued*)

4. What gets measured gets done.

5. Ruthlessly focus on your priorities.

6. The humble leader wins in the medium to long term.

7. Be self-aware; you're a shadow-caster.

8. Look in the mirror to account for mistakes and out the window to assign credit.

9. Invest most of your management time with your best people.

10. Hire the best people possible, patiently.

Lead from Behind and Use the Hot Seat

A good leader has to have deft emotional intelligence and really *hear* what people are saying, even if they're not saying it directly. You also have to be willing to dig deeper, push the extremes, and have uncomfortable conversations. You also have to be willing to make mistakes. That's what separates a leader from simply a manager.

One leadership tactic we both like is to lead from behind. This is driven by the old adage of teaching people how to fish instead of giving them a fish. We put our people in the hot seat frequently to help them prepare for meetings or presentations. That's a great example of how we lead from behind. We'll be in the meeting with them for support, but they have to drive it themselves. As alignment pushes you to collaborate more frequently, your teams are also going to be in that hot seat more often. Preparing them for it helps with the transition.

There are a lot of younger people—Millennials, as they're called—in the early years of their marketing careers who aren't prepared for the typical salesperson's assertiveness. It's intimidating and it sometimes pushes people to be awkward in their communication or make bad decisions. If we can teach them how to explain their actions, provide context, and detail the thought that went into a decision, they can have a successful discussion.

The hot seat concept also helps people learn how to take criticism, and that's especially useful for marketing folks. Sales reps are always in the hot seat. They're constantly being challenged by customers in tense meetings and being questioned by managers on forecast calls. It's part of the sales job to be good and calm under pressure.

Practicing scenarios where you prepare people for that tension is a great exercise. It also helps them anticipate questions, which is helpful for more junior members of the team who don't yet know what a CEO or VP will ask. It shows them the importance of preparation, having background information, and knowing how their projects might impact other teams across the company.

Are Millennials Born to Be Aligned?

If you're reading this book, you're probably somewhere in the middle or later part of your career. We hate to admit it, but we're well outside of that all-powerful 18-to-35-year-old age group. That means we're a generation removed from those eager, bright, fresh college grads who are entering the workforce with new attitudes, new ways of working, and new expectations on everything from management styles to technology.

It also means we should probably have a serious talk about the younger generation. You know, those kids with the different hair, who listen to that loud music, who say things that just make you want to scream, "GET OFF MY LAWN!" Oh wait! We were those kids not so long ago. And we're sure some business books back in the 90s made it a point to explain how to manage the slackers of Gen X, what with our grunge music and disdain for authority.

What's clear is that those new to the workforce—whether it's 2016 or 1986—see things differently than those whose tenure is measured in decades. But instead of trying to explain how this new generation of Millennials thinks about their

(Continued)

(*Continued*)

careers, we'll let one of them explain. Esther Costa is a member of the college graduating class of 2013 and is in the early stages of her marketing career.

"It's a challenge being at the bottom," Esther lamented. "When you're just out of school, you have no idea of corporate life. It was eye opening. It was like, 'Oh, I see it now. The customer is the banana in the banana split!' It was fun to start to put things together from a business sense."

Everyone starts his or her career at the bottom; that's nothing new. It's the shifting attitudes that shape how different generations approach challenges and each other that have changed. Millennials' preference for being recognized for their work seems to differ from older generations, and it reflects the oft-talked-about everybody-gets-a-trophy syndrome. Millennials grew up in a time when, regardless of achievement, everyone was recognized for their contribution. Entering a merit-based workforce is an adjustment for both the Millennials and their managers.

"We frequently think about the recognition we're going to get from it and how long it's going to take to get to that point," Esther explained. "We worry about smaller things, and wonder if every little step is being watched and if it's going to matter in our careers. If a higher-up accepts the recognition [we feel we are due], it causes issues. You become very aware that you are low on the stack and you have to work hard to get the recognition.

"But being raised in an era of shared success has made it easier for Millennials to work together, with collaboration being the norm. In essence, giving everyone a trophy has fostered the notion that everyone is an important part of the team and all contributions combine to make for a better result.

"We like to learn from our mistakes, but it's harder to make mistakes when we're pushed down a path because that's the way it's been done before," added Esther. "I'm not naïve and I know that I'm inexperienced. But not having the experience,

> and putting a bunch of our minds together, lets us come up with new and creative solutions."
>
> With that perspective on collaboration, it's Millennials who might be the biggest drivers of corporate-wide alignment over the next few years.
>
> "We're still trying to figure out why there isn't any alignment," Esther says. "It may have always been this way, but why? It should be better, and maybe we're just too inexperienced to understand why it won't work. But that could also be what makes it work. We're a little bit more optimistic, I think. Maybe that's inexperience, but maybe it's also a new attitude that sales and marketing should be working together on everything."

Mary Shea, a principal analyst at Forrester Research, co-authored a February 2016 report titled, "May The Force Of The Millennials Be With You!" In it, Forrester proffers that, while Baby Boomers are consistent, loyal, and individualistic, technology has pushed Millennials to be more entrepreneurial, adaptive, and collaborative. In turn, those characteristics have changed the makeup of the newest crop of sales reps. The authors state in the report that "Millennials are well positioned to have advantages over more tenured sales professionals with regard to leveraging technology to help drive efficiencies and uncover insights." In other words, Gen Xers and Boomers need to get on the tech train or get out of the way!

What Makes a Good Leader in an Aligned Organization?

A good leader is a good leader. But in an aligned organization, the profile is a bit different. While the skills that took you to the top are mostly the same, the skills required to excel through alignment are a bit unique. Of course, collaboration and cooperation are key, but so are experience, empathy, and a broader knowledge of the other domain or a willingness to learn it. You need to be intellectually curious and inquisitive.

Aligned leaders show an understanding for others' discipline and process, and they have strong examples to prove it. In other words, they have knowledge *and* credibility. There's also a need for intellectual curiosity and for understanding the evolving nature of the counterpart department's work. We've talked about marketing becoming more technology-driven and sales moving toward new selling methods, such as social selling. Leaders will recognize, understand, and respond to the changing nature of their counterpart's discipline.

For example, a great sales leader can explain how account-based everything works, how marketing automation and CRM are integrated, and why marketing focuses on certain metrics. Conversely, a great marketing leader can explain in detail how their sales cycle progresses; discuss average deal sizes, win rates, and quota attainment; and also understand the biggest challenges to sales effectiveness. This level of understanding fosters trust and respect from both your leadership peers as well as your own and other teams. It also helps you collaborate as you problem solve and dig into the details of why something isn't working.

All of this leads to better communication. A great leader understands the concepts and challenges and granular points that their counterpart is discussing. They use the right terminology and talk with empathy for the other's responsibilities. (Remember this even as you interview potential leaders to be sure they are answering questions or giving examples from past roles that reflect a deep empathy for their counterpart and the challenges they face.)

Another point to remember is that collusion can be a good thing. We both use that word frequently to underscore the power we have when we work together. If one of us asks our CEO for more budget or more people, we need to make an understandably strong argument. But if we both approach our CEO with a joint request, he is going to have a tough time turning us down. It also works within our teams. If Tracy needs more effort from the sales team on a specific campaign, Andrea asks her reps what they are doing to make the campaign more successful. It also works to protect each other from short-term hiccups or unexpected weak performance. Having the support of an aligned colleague can have an extraordinary effect throughout the company. But, as usual, there's much, much more to being a good executive in an aligned organization.

What Makes a Good CMO?

We think the best CMOs are triple threats who have the following:

1. **Domain expertise**, meaning they have a background in the product or service you're selling. For example, a software CMO has a technical background while a manufacturing CMO might have engineering or production experience.

2. **Superior marketing creativity**. The CMO is the visionary and sets the tone of the brand. Being outwardly creative is how to attract followers, both in the market and in sales.

3. **Analytic skills and business acumen**, meaning a CMO is a master of key marketing and sales analytics, can read a balance sheet, hold his or her own on a sales forecast call, and navigate the business politics inside a key customer. You also know how to draw insight from analysis and how to apply it.

A CMO's creativity has to also be combined with a natural curiosity and a willingness to experiment. There are so many ways for marketers to inexpensively try new things these days, from small email campaigns to self-produced videos to writing a controversial blog post. That willingness to push and try is not only how you discover new opportunities, it's how you excite and motivate your teams. When sales sees a CMO who is willing to go outside of the box to fill the funnel, they'll have more respect for that person and benefit from more success, which will result in tighter alignment. A sure sign of pending failure is a CMO who simply brings their playbook from their last company and tries to apply it at their new company.

This triple threat is becoming more important, not only for alignment, but in general. Marketing has expanded so much in recent years that the CMO is overseeing a wider range of people, skillsets, and domains.

Umberto Milletti, InsideView's CEO, has said that the CMO holds "the broadest role in any company . . . outside of the CEO."

The CMOs also need to fight to prove their worth to a skeptical sales team. Kerry Barrett is the CEO of Accretive Solutions, a professional services firm, and she has seen how an undervalued marketing team can quickly be relegated to simply producing content and running campaigns.

"The CMO, and even the CEO, has to ensure that marketing has a seat at the table," Kerry says. "It's the CMO's job to make sure that marketing is heard. When sales thinks that marketing just doesn't get it, that marketing can't sell, that widens the rift. It takes a strong CMO to break down those barriers, work with sales, get closer with customers, and show that they understand how difficult sales can be. Then marketing can show they are an ally of sales, and can fill the blind spots that sales might have."

Laura Ramos, VP and principal analyst at Forrester Research, authored a March 2015 report titled, "From Priming the Pipeline to Engaging Buyers: The B2B CMO's New Role in Sales Enablement." In it, she asked B2B CMOs what was the most important thing they could do to help sales succeed. Here are the top five, which you should use as a checklist to evaluate your own priorities:

1. Increase the productivity of customer/opportunity acquisition.
2. Target the right accounts and help sales pursue them.
3. Develop the right content to increase brand awareness.
4. Supply sales with tools to frame conversations in customer terms.
5. Bring customers together to explore topics and educate.

Another huge asset for any CMO is the respect to be gained from having had sales experience at some point in their career. The additional credibility and respect gained from a sales team who values firsthand experience cannot be replicated. It's not required, however, and Tracy points out that while she's never carried a bag, she's had a close connection to her sales counterparts in every company she's been in. While she has not been a seller, she does have empathy. She's always listened to sales to understand the struggles that they're having.

Tracy's empathy for sales reps began when she was just 16 years old. Her father was a marketing executive in a large software company and his sales counterparts frequently visited their home to socialize. Tracy heard them commiserating over their busy travel schedules, stressful negotiations, and constant pressure to hit quotas. She not only felt empathy for their struggles, but she also sensed a business opportunity and became a personal assistant for several of them. For $100 a month, she ran errands, bought groceries, picked up dry cleaning, and generally helped them keep their lives going while they were constantly traveling. It helped guide her impression of salespeople not as sharks, but as people with overwhelming demands.

What Makes a Good Sales VP?

It's uncommon for sales executives to have marketing experience and it's rare that candidates for sales leadership roles are asked about marketing in a job interview. In an aligned organization, understanding how a sales leader will engage with marketing is a key consideration, but you can't assume that alignment is on every candidate's agenda. Sales VP's have to understand marketing and how to work effectively with their counterpart in that department. Marketing can't be expected to fall in line behind the sales leader—and the consequences of doing so would be detrimental to both teams and the company.

Andrea worked on trade shows and events and launched new products into the market early in her career, all of which are traditional domains of marketing. Having had that experience has helped Andrea understand what goes into marketing: the importance of messaging consistency, the value of giveaways, and the timing of launching into the general market.

As with the broadening scope of the CMO role, the sales VP job description is bursting. There's more of an operational focus on scalability and creating a complex engine of sales growth that covers inbound sales, outbound sales, field sales, inside sales, channel sales, customer success, and more. This demands even more collaboration and alignment with marketing, since growth isn't easy without marketing's support and marketing has to support more and more sales specialization.

What's becoming obviously less attractive in a sales leader is the maverick attitude, which creates a dynamic where sales is the aggressor and marketing is the subordinate. Alignment requires an enlightened sales leader, one who's smart enough to know that everyone can be more successful with marketing's support.

If You Do Nothing Else About Leadership, Do These Things

1. Honestly evaluate your own skills and consider filling in or hiring where you have gaps. Accept that you can't do it alone and make a list of what that means to you. Check your ego at the door. Be comfortable accepting that you don't have all of the answers.

2. Take an alignment-promoting action in your next meeting. Extend trust to your counterpart. Watch your body language and tone of voice when meetings get tense. Look for your triggers and note what you do when they appear, then think about how you might do it differently.

3. Always be ready to be wrong and have a strategy for when you are. Don't think about it as admitting weakness, think of it as strengthening relationships and building trust. Go over a few scenarios in your head so you're prepared.

4. Seek to gain skills outside of your domain. Volunteer for side projects that give you exposure to other areas. If you're in marketing, consider a role as a sales rep. If you're in sales, offer to help with marketing campaigns and event planning.

5. Get exposed to customers as much as possible. Volunteer to make customer satisfaction or net promoter survey calls. Offer to make cold sales calls for a few hours each week. Have lunch with a customer.

Chapter 5

Data Is the Great Equalizer of Alignment

Data is everywhere and every day more is being generated, collected, and analyzed. It's been estimated that 90 percent of the world's *total* data has been generated in just the past two years. So much new data is being created that we now refer to it as *big data* to reflect the massive mountains collected by our increasingly watchful technologies.

Data is also, without a doubt, a gold mine for sales and marketing. Since B2B buyers now conduct most of the purchasing process on their own, they are doing more online. That's good, because it lets us collect more and more information about their activity. This data allows us to get inside the heads of prospects, see exactly what they are doing and when, and make detailed assumptions about their intent and likely next moves. It can tell us which lead is ready to buy, which customer is ready to defect, or which sales rep is ready for an uncomfortable conversation with their manager.

Where data can get us into trouble is when we blindly trust it, when we treat sales and marketing—and business in general—as a pure science instead of an artful, or even gut-driven process.

Moneyball, the popular book and subsequent movie, dramatized the success of running a baseball team based on player data, even if it defied conventional wisdom. Data geeks, such as popular statistician Nate Silver, founder and editor of ESPN's FiveThirtyEight blog, have further popularized the ever-widening role of data in our lives. Now, new roles such as data scientist and marketing technologist are popping up in business.

In the age of big data, marketing from the gut is considered an obstacle to success. Big data has been held up as the potential savior of all business ills—but how far from the truth that is.

Data is a resource that can drive our businesses, to be sure, but it's up to us to make the decisions. Data always tells us something, but it never tells us what to do. That's where we humans come in, to discern the insights hidden in the data.

Data, especially *big* data, is also full of distractions and noise, and more data is not always better. A reliance on data tends to eliminate conversations and collaboration. Marketing, for example, has data on every touchpoint with a prospect, so they may not see a need to talk with sales about their tactics. If the data says X, then X it is. Why involve sales? Or why even talk to a customer?

The bigness of data has helped drive a wedge between sales and marketing. And more data is coming.

More Data from More Sources

Marketing and sales each depend, independently, on their biggest data tools: marketing automation and CRM. Over the years, these have become fairly easily integrated. Contact data entered into an online form generated by your marketing automation tool is typically transferred to your CRM system. Similarly, if inside sales calls a contact who asks to never be contacted again, that piece of unsubscribe data is typically transferred back to your marketing automation tool.

But when there are more systems to manage, more data appears. Maybe you use HubSpot to manage social media, WordPress to manage your blog, a content management system (CMS) to manage downloadable assets, sales software for deal acceleration, and another social selling tool. It doesn't take much to add adjacent systems, but it does take some work and planning to integrate all of that data. Based on our experience at different companies, and especially with our current customers, integration rarely happens until there's a major problem.

Just take social media, for example. Social media's ubiquity and reach create a huge potential opportunity for companies today. Marketing can reach millions of people in real time for no cost and they can create hyper-targeted messages that resonate with a tiny sub-sub-segment of a lucrative market. Sales can take the reins and use social selling to initiate direct, immediate, and one-to-one contact with a hot lead in little more than 140 characters. It's fast, simple, free, and they don't have to ask IT or marketing for approval.

All of these reach advantages introduce potential downsides and additional friction between sales and marketing. Touchpoints get lost or overlap. Strategies become diluted or diverge. More data has to be captured, analyzed, and interpreted. The fact that anyone *can* use it and everyone *is* using it means that sales reps are connecting with prospects whenever they want while marketing tries, in vain, to control the message.

More Data Does Not Mean Better Alignment

The massive move to cloud-based software has also added to our data problems. Whereas IT used to be the common set of eyes on every piece of software rolled out within an enterprise, now all it takes is a credit card and a manager's approval. There's no longer a strategic, company-wide view of technology solutions, let alone coordination between sales and marketing. Data integration isn't considered and the data silos that were the bane of businesses in the early 2000s are popping up all over again.

"If your data is siloed, you're increasing the amount of data you have with each system but you're only incrementally increasing your ability to execute—or you even drag it down," says John Donlon, a research director at SiriusDecisions, a global B2B research and advisory firm. "It takes too many cycles to try to pull all of the information together." (See Figure 5.1.)

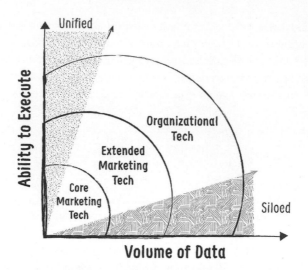

FIGURE 5.1 John Donlon, research director at SiriusDecisions, developed a concept stating the ability to execute is directly correlated to how well integrated your different data systems are, with more siloed data holding back your ability to execute.

"Fifty-eight percent of organizations indicate poor alignment between sales operations and marketing operations," he says. "We see four main areas causing that misalignment: planning, lead management, measurement, and data management. For data management, it comes down to poor data quality and an inability to integrate data. To achieve true alignment, you need to bring that data together, and when you do, the insight you can attain—and in turn, the impact on executing marketing activities—goes through the roof!"

All of these great technological advancements add up to one thing: more misalignment. In today's B2B selling environment, both sales and marketing can engage with the same opportunity at the same time, but with different messages and no coordination.

While sales is chatting with a lead on Twitter about their product needs, marketing is emailing the same lead information about services. While marketing has a prospect in a nurturing campaign, sales is working on a price quote for a conversation made via a LinkedIn group.

The consequence? A diluted, disjointed, customer experience; inefficiencies; lost opportunities for your company; and low productivity for your teams. Sales and marketing alignment is your only solution, but first you have to manage your data.

Defining Sales and Marketing Data

Data comes in many forms and from many sources. Here, we're talking about sales and marketing data, which is the data you collect about your prospects, leads, and customers. It takes several forms, which we term *data, insights*, and *connections* (Figure 5.2).

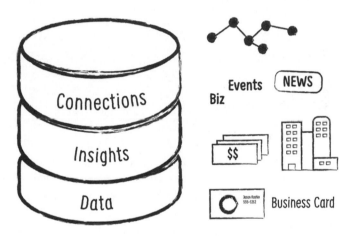

FIGURE 5.2   There are many different types of data and all are important pieces of the alignment puzzle.

Data

At the base level, there's the simple *data* you collect from and about your prospects. It's easy to gather—you could even buy it—and allows you to quickly segment prospects into rough groups. The names and phone numbers marketing collects on web forms or at an event fall into this category, as does the

(*Continued*)

(*Continued*)

company revenue number the sales team adds later in the process.

A decade ago, this was valuable data that companies treated like gold. Today, it's table stakes.

Data is enriched by sales and marketing. You collect it via various means as prospects continue their journey. This enriched data is even more valuable and a competitive advantage to your company. What you know about a prospect is now going beyond what any of your competitors can find. It's knowing which keyword drove them to your website, which white papers they downloaded, which product pages they viewed, or which blog posts they read. It might also be data to add industry codes, financials, and the updated company employee count.

Insights

The third layer goes beyond structured names and numbers and encompasses what is called *unstructured* data. Think of it as information that can't be easily collected automatically; a person needs to discern it. This could include notes a sales rep adds about a prospect's key business partners, recent (and relevant) business events, the names of champions and key executives, or business attributes that impact your dealings with them. For example, the prospect does business globally, so your currency hedging service might be of interest to them. If they lease all of their real estate, your property management services would *not* be interesting to them. If they just won a big deal, they may be required to source more components.

This is the type of data that requires some research and interpretation to draw meanings. These are *insights*, and they may be fleeting. They also require a human—at least for now—to understand and assign relevance.

Insights build your competitive advantage and your ability to win more deals, engage faster, and target better. It includes financials, like the trajectory of the prospect's stock price, or the fact that they are a potential acquisition target. It could also include news, like the prospect's opening of a new production facility.

Insights increase the value of your data, but they require interpretation to separate the signals from the noise.

Connections

Finally, the fourth layer of data is connections. This is a very human concept, but data abounds to help you find and leverage your connections to others. Connection data also offers an unrivaled competitive advantage.

We all know that cold calls have extremely low conversion rates. A Baylor University study found that cold calling has a 0.3 percent success rate on appointments per call, meaning you'd have to make roughly 300 cold calls to schedule a single appointment.

We also know that warm referrals—being introduced to a prospect by a mutual acquaintance—increases those odds significantly. InsideView ran a survey that found that 84 percent of B2B sellers listed a personal connection or warm introduction as *the number one most helpful* way for sales reps to get through the prospect's door.

Facebook and LinkedIn can show you how you are connected—and how to get introduced—to nearly anyone on earth. Newer services even let you see how your *colleagues* are connected to your prospects. Seeing and leveraging the data of connections is how today's sales process begins.

Data Is the Currency of Growth

When we say data, we recognize that it is so much more than contacts and company sizes, and can come from many different sources. Data provides the insights that impact everything you do. It's a strategic asset and it should be treated that way.

Think of it this way: Data is the currency that B2B companies use to buy growth. We'd like to take credit for that idea, but it's from an April 2016 Forrester Research report, "A Customer-Obsessed Operating Model Demands A Close Partnership With Your CIO." In it, they state, "Data is the currency of the digital age. With the right data—potentially combining your data with data from other personal value ecosystem players—you can create new sources of customer value."

If you want to maximize the value of your data, sales and marketing have to treat data as a common language that we both agree upon and share. It's constantly changing, so maintaining one common, shared system makes both our jobs easier.

Making the "Single Source of Truth" Cliché a Reality

There's a cliché around data that says you need a *single source of truth*. For sales and marketing, we see this from two perspectives. First, both teams need visibility across all of the data along the entire customer journey. Second, both teams need to agree on a tiebreaker data source.

We have already discussed visibility and the importance of sharing data across the customer's journey. Sales can more effectively engage when they see what marketing has learned, and marketing can better target by using what sales has learned to hone messaging, for instance.

A tiebreaker system is a bit less obvious, but it means agreeing on which system will determine which attribute is correct. For example, say there's a big opportunity and your mid-market sales team, who covers companies with revenue below $100 million, is fighting with the enterprise team for ownership. Marketing's data shows the lead's revenue as $112 million, while sales' data shows it as $86 million, creating obvious confusion. A tiebreaker system would determine the true revenue. In this case, the revenue value from a trusted, third-party tiebreaker system would be used to route the lead.

Building your single source of truth uses a combination of shared data and a tiebreaker system.

Begin with a Data Audit

The best starting point for building an aligned data strategy is to perform an audit of all data-gathering tools used by both sales and marketing. Find out how many are being used, what's installed but not being used, and which systems are critical versus marginally useful. Look into where tools are integrated or not, what data is being exchanged, and where gaps are being created.

As you're mapping your data and systems to your customer engagement model, investigate the data that is or isn't being transferred at each handoff point. You'll be surprised by the amount of data being collected compared with how much is being shared.

Throughout the audit think about each dataset's value beyond just the data itself. How accurate is the data? Is it current? How does it fit into the customer's journey? Is it actionable?

You'll want to measure each tool or system or database by the value of the data. If the data is inaccurate, out of date, or of limited use, you may want to scrap it altogether. At some point more data becomes a distraction and can cloud the view and value of the useful data. But how do you determine the value of data? We're glad you asked.

Do It Right: Create a Data Strategy and Track Its Maturation

Tim Thorpe is director of digital marketing, global marketing, and communications at Black & Veatch, a global engineering and construction firm. He leads the company's strategy for sales and marketing data and knows firsthand the challenges involved.

"The biggest challenge revolves around where that data comes from, because it's in many different places," Tim says. "It's websites, notepads, emails, business cards, email signature lines, spreadsheets—there's really no end to the different data sources. The variety of places data comes from—that's the number-one challenge.

"The second challenge, if you really want to have a successful data strategy, is that you must have a data quality process

(Continued)

(*Continued*)

that sits between all those disparate sources and your internal systems. How do you have a quality process that is also efficient for your business? There is no easy solution. When you talk about efficiency and quality, there's a trade-off. You want to minimize the time requirements to manage data but then quality may drop. There always has to be a balance between quality and efficiency in business."

"What you can do with your data eventually reflects your organization's marketing and sales maturity," added Fredrik Winterlind, vice president of global marketing and communication at Black & Veatch.

"When you report on activity, like number of events managed, you are at the lowest marketing maturity level but you're on your way," Fredrik explained. "When you can predict revenue lost from potential defections and you can raise a flag to a future purchase, then you are at a high maturity level. That's driven by how well you manage your data.

"If you're in marketing, you know you always need to focus on business value," Fredrik continued. "When you stop talking about marketing's impact on web traffic and start talking about marketing's impact on revenue, you get the ear of other executives. The more mature your data strategy, the more you can rely on it to create business value."

Determining Data's Value

In the opening of this chapter, we talked about how more and more data is being created and collected. Not all of it is useful, however. In fact, some data is noise—or it's flat-out wrong.

As you evaluate all of your tools, look at every accompanying dataset from these four perspectives: accuracy, currency, context, and actionability (Figure 5.3).

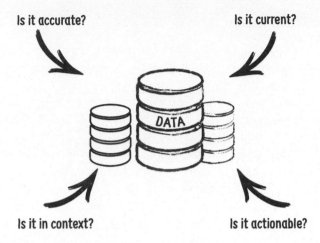

Is it accurate?

Is it current?

DATA

Is it in context?

Is it actionable?

FIGURE 5.3 Look at your data and ask these questions to begin determining its value and what you need to do to increase that value.

Is the Data Accurate?

According to SiriusDecisions, the average B2B database is 25 percent inaccurate at any given time. They also found that more than 80 percent of marketing records lack company size in terms of both number of employees and revenue. That's an enormous gap and a severe impediment to sales and marketing productivity.

Accuracy is more than just correctness. When looking at an email address, you want to be sure it is correct. As you move up a level to a contact's full record (their *business card*, if you will), accuracy also conveys completeness. Be sure you have all of the data you need about a contact and their company to help sales and marketing be effective.

Having multiple data sources can help with accuracy. The concepts of triangulation and intelligent aggregation mean pulling data from different sources and going with the value that is most agreed upon. For example, if one source says a company has 500 employees and four other trusted sources all say 625, triangulation assumes that 625 is the accurate value.

Inaccurate and incomplete data cause the same issues. If a data field in a contact record is blank, it's just as useless as if it were wrong.

Is the Data Current?

Several studies, including one from Harte Hanks, a marketing services company, and another by John M. Coe, co-founder and principal of B2BMarketing.com, a consulting and data services company, and the author of *The Fundamentals of Business-to-Business Sales & Marketing*, put the "decay rate" of B2B data at between 60 and 70 percent per year. Why so significant? Because people change jobs, companies move locations and introduce new products, and businesses are acquired.

All data is fluid, whether it's a company's revenue number, a compelling business event, or a contact's email address. Data is a flowing river, constantly changing. If you take a snapshot (e.g., build a list, segment accounts, assign territories, etc.), the data has changed since that snapshot was taken. Data can help you win a deal today but be worthless tomorrow.

A report by PayScale, a salary, benefits, and compensation information company, showed the median employee tenure at some larger companies was well below 18 months. Google's median tenure was 1.1 years at the time, while Ross Stores' was 1.2 years and New York Life Insurance's was 1.4 years. With large companies across different industries seeing that frequency of turnover, the people you're targeting today are probably moving around much more than you might expect.

That is data decay. Unless you keep your data current, it's getting less useful every day. Again, think of data as a river changing every instance. The data you have right now is just a snapshot in time. It's up to you to determine how current your data has to be for your unique business. We've found that, regardless of your business or industry, a major goal to strive for is having data that is current to at least the most recent quarter.

In What Context Is the Data Useful?

Context is how you pull data together to create new and novel insights. Adding social media data to company news, for example, might uncover trends or signals that may have been missed when looking at single data sources. Today's modern data—social, networks, connections—can all be used to add context to your other data.

The human brain is critical here. Context generally has to be interpreted. For example, knowing that a lead downloaded your product data sheet today is marginally useful. But also knowing that, within the past week, they looked at your services web page and visited your blog post on your company's financing options likely signals that they are very close to a buying decision.

For example, your web analytics or marketing automation tool can alert you when a lead visits your website more than three times in a seven-day period. That data is undoubtedly useful, but you can significantly increase its value by adding the context of what they are viewing, what they've viewed before, and what your experience tells you.

Imagine if you knew what all the interactions were across all the key people in an account. You could see how engaged your company was with that prospect, looking at contact with all decision makers across the board. Increasingly, companies are buying from cross-functional groups of people—making your life even harder. This is the crux of account-based marketing, and we'll talk about this more in Chapter 8.

Remember that data is just an indicator. People make the decisions. If you are missing part of the data, don't have the full context, or are working from old data, you may make the wrong decisions.

Is the Data Actionable?

Good data gives you a better ability to separate the signals from the noise. Noise delays your actions while true signals prompt you to take an action. In the context of sales and marketing alignment, an *action* is, at a fundamental level, the steps you take toward closing or disqualifying a lead.

Unfortunately, actionable data doesn't appear on its own. Our earlier points of accuracy, recency, and context all combine to help you determine a data point's actionability. Consider the following example to see how important it is that you fully understand actionability. Suppose you call a lead and assume they have the budget for your products because their last-quarter earnings were great. On the call, the lead tells you that news just broke that they lost two big customers last week. Or, maybe instead, you learn that the prospect's major priorities have changed. While your data on their earnings was accurate, it wasn't recent so it isn't actionable.

Your objectives also help define actionability. Do you want to close bigger deals, enter a new industry, increase upsells, or simply move leads closer to a purchase? Your objectives can change the definition of an actionable data point as they become more focused. If marketing's objective is to bring in more leads, then every new lead is actionable. If marketing's objective is to bring in more construction industry leads, then only a subset of leads are actionable. Of course, to make that determination, you need to know every lead's industry, and that means having accurate and complete data today and tomorrow.

Maintaining Your Data's Health

At InsideView, among our many other services, we provide data, insights, and connections on target companies and the people in them. We frequently talk about data maintenance as though your data is a living, breathing entity. We mention your data's health, we talk about best practices in data hygiene, and we advise you to evaluate your data's cleanliness. You want your data to perform at its highest potential. To do so, it needs to be in tip-top shape and you need a training plan to get there.

Think about how you would approach your own health and fitness. Imagine you wanted to run a marathon. You wouldn't just hop off the couch and run 26.2 miles. You'd need to assess your current health, make sure you're fit enough to take on such a goal, and then put together a customized training program that involves workouts, nutrition, and more.

Just like your own health, data health isn't a one-time activity. It's not that simple for either our bodies or for your data. If you're healthy enough to run a marathon today, but eat donuts and surf the web every day starting tomorrow, you won't be in marathon shape for very long.

As we mentioned earlier, data that's accurate today slowly degrades over time. If you magically make your data 100 percent current and accurate today, it will be less and less so starting tomorrow. Data health is an ongoing effort that takes commitment and planning.

Now let's show you how to get your sales and marketing data in shape and maintain its fitness.

Establish Your Starting Point

Your first step in assessing and maintaining your data's health is to diagnose the accuracy and completeness of your customer data so you know your starting point. This is like hopping on the scale or taking your resting heart rate or timing a one-mile run on the first day of your new marathon training routine. Setting your baseline helps you know where to focus your efforts, helps you track your progress, and gives you an indication of how much work needs to be done to reach your goal.

One way to evaluate the current health of your data is to benchmark a sample set of data and understand just how out-of-shape it really is. You can use an automated data service to compare a set of random records to what's in the database or you can survey your sales reps to ask how often they run into bad data. You can even look at your marketing email bounce rates to see what percentage of outdated email addresses are in your database.

You're not looking for a smoking gun or a way to assign blame. You simply want to know how healthy your data is today and get some indication of where to focus and how much effort is going to be required.

Clean Your House First

Your second step is to clean up your current data. In this step, you want to identify and correct inaccurate data, remove duplicates, and complete missing fields.

But, just like stretching before you go on a training run, data cleanliness has to become a routine. Many services exist to help you keep your data clean and current. We recommend using such a service at least every six months after the initial cleaning, but quarterly is best.

You want to exit this step confident that your data is ready to serve as the foundation for your alignment initiative. You don't want claims of incomplete or inaccurate sales and marketing data to become a scapegoat for other alignment challenges. Getting your data in shape gives you the confidence to act on it when it matters most.

Supplement Your Data

Top athletes like to enrich their diets with such things as vitamins, wheatgrass, and flax seeds. Even weekend warriors grab coconut water or the latest electrolyte-filled fitness drink after a workout. Why? Because it helps you recover more quickly and gives you the nutrients you lost during exercise. Just like supplements enrich your intake of vitamins and minerals, your intake of *data* benefits from enrichment as well.

In the previous step, you cleaned up your existing database. Seconds later, a new prospect visited your website and entered their name, email address, and company name into a form. All of a sudden, you have a new, but incomplete, lead in your database.

Supplementing your data, which we call *data enrichment*, means adding missing data as new prospects enter your CRM or marketing automation systems. It also means correcting and appending information as it changes over time. Many data enrichment services exist and some even plug directly into your existing software tools so data is constantly and automatically enriched.

Data enrichment not only helps sales quickly connect with the right contacts, but it also helps marketing target more accurately and effectively by providing more, and more granular, data for each prospect.

Switch It Up

It's boring to have a fitness routine that follows the same cycle every day. The CrossFit craze, which gives participants a new and varied routine each day, is a great example of the power of fitness variety. In training for a marathon, it's not good to run the same route every day and leave it at that. Many marathoners do strength training between running days; some run sprint intervals one day and slower, long distance routes the next. Variety helps you continue to improve.

Variety also helps your sales and marketing efforts by adding new prospects to your campaigns and programs. Attending a tradeshow in a new industry or sponsoring a third-party event are typical ways to add new leads to your database. Purchasing highly targeted lists of new prospects can also expand your total addressable market, but that's sometimes a risky proposition because those lists can be filled with bad data. If you go that route, be sure you're acquiring fresh data from a reputable vendor who can back up their claims of accuracy and relevancy.

You'll want to frequently add new data to keep your database fresh and add new prospects as older prospects become stale, lost, or less viable. Both sales and marketing will benefit as you add new data from outside of your internal programs.

Add More Depth with Insights and Connections

Earlier in this chapter, we talked about the layers of data: data, insights, and connections. With data fitness, you're mainly focused on the data layer, specifically names and numbers. Where your data really becomes more valuable and actionable is with insights and connections.

Insights are *news that you can use*. They give marketing and sales the power they need to effectively engage or more quickly reach out. Insights include breaking news about companies you are pursuing or alerts on a contact's role change.

Connections make it easier to engage with the decision makers that sales is trying to reach. This data layer reveals that your CFO went to business school with your lead's director of finance or that your former manager now holds a director-level job at a new prospect.

Nearly everyone on your sales and marketing team already has their own networks on Facebook, Twitter, LinkedIn, and other social and professional networks. Tapping into those networks can magnify the value of connections and share it across your organization.

Combining data, insights, and connections adds up to an unbeatable force. Knowing whom to call on is just the tip of the proverbial iceberg. Knowing who they are, their current business needs, how you can engage, and who can connect you puts you in the lead.

Keep Your Data in Shape

We've said it a few times, but it warrants repeating. Data fitness isn't a won-and-done effort. Data is accurate today, but inaccuracy starts tomorrow. And just as data is constantly changing, the business of data is changing as well.

A decade ago, the concept of moving your data and your software to the cloud was scoffed at. People thought it would never become mainstream. Companies wondered why they would ever put their valuable company and customer data under someone else's roof. Now, it's almost a disadvantage to own software.

We see data and data services evolving as well. One new concept specifically related to data fitness is *records under management*. Think of this as outsourcing your data management, kind of like getting a personal trainer. You still own the data, but someone else stores it, cleans it, and keeps it in shape. All you have to do is pay for the service.

Keep an open mind when new markets and services pop up that could help you improve your data's value while lowering your its resource requirements.

Take Responsibility for Your Data

Data is critical to successful sales and marketing alignment. Don't treat it as an afterthought or a distraction or simply a tool. Build your strategy around it, improve it where there are gaps, and keep it performing at optimal levels.

Data management is a responsibility jointly owned by sales and marketing. You need to push data breadth, quality, and management as a fundamental component of business success. It's also a good catalyst for alignment, because data is concrete. It exists. You can point to what you have and everyone in sales and marketing will have an opinion about how good (or bad) your data currently is.

By joining together and being aligned on goals, sales and marketing can better motivate operations and IT to make data a priority. If not, sales and marketing can build the case for moving forward anyway. Tying the importance of data to revenue growth should make this easy.

Get It Right: Hire a Personal Trainer for Your Data

Alex Shipillo directs demand generation at Influitive, an advocate marketing software company that helps B2B companies harness customer enthusiasm for use in marketing and sales efforts. Alex saw data as the key to helping Influitive capture more opportunities, but they didn't have the expertise or man power to focus specifically on data. So, Alex hired a data intelligence manager and Influitive has since seen a significant impact on their business. "Before, we tended to forget about data and how it could improve sales and marketing results," Alex explained. "Now, it's always discussed. The impact has been quite significant. We now have the attitude that data always improves the outcome, and can always benefit us down the road."

Influitive's data intelligence managerworks tightly with sales operations and marketing operations. Together, the three form what Alex calls their *revenue operations team.*

"It's like a three-legged stool," says Alex. "We have three very competent people who now have deep discussions about our cross-functional data issues, everything from changing fields in our CRM system to finding data to help make strategic decisions. They all work together to solve problems, and it's helped to improve communications between the broader sales and marketing teams."

Prior to hiring a data intelligence manager, Alex explains, sales operations and marketing operations were less connected. Now, working together, they dive into problems and propose solutions as a group, taking into account their various points of view.

Finding a dedicated data intelligence manager wasn't easy, according to Alex. The right person needed marketing skills as well as data skills—but that wasn't all. "We wanted a hacky data person first, who was a marketer second," explains Alex.

(Continued)

(Continued)

"The right candidate had to be able to write scripts and process large amounts of data across multiple systems. But we didn't want him or her to just fulfill requests for data and reports. We wanted someone genuinely curious. We expected the person to be very collaborative and come in with big thinking, eager to do lots of brainstorming."

Alex sees data operations becoming more of its own domain as companies continue to use data as a source of value and growth. While marketing ops and sales ops roles will continue to expand and change, having someone focus deeply on data is becoming more critical. And, as Alex notes, it's also critical to deepening the alignment between sales and marketing.

"The wall between marketing and sales is breaking down, especially as we rely on each other to achieve the greater business goals," Alex added. "It's less about those two teams battling and more about collaborating. Collaboration lets us make better, faster improvements to our business, regardless of who is doing the executing."

Data's Role Across the Customer Journey

Data impacts the entire customer journey. As you're working to map the path of your company's customers, you'll start to see handoffs between sales and marketing, and maybe other groups. And as you audit the tools used by sales and marketing, you'll see where data is collected and discover where it is and isn't being shared. These are the opportunities that start to build closer alignment between sales and marketing (Figure 5.4).

When marketing sees how they can benefit from visibility into previously unknown sales data, they will start to see lightbulbs go off. When sales learns how some previously unknown marketing data could've helped them in a recent deal, they'll want more visibility right away. Mapping where data is collected, via which tools, and

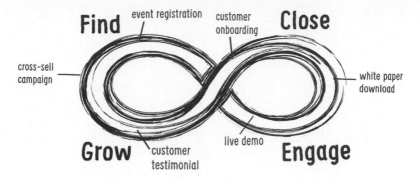

FIGURE 5.4 In the modern customer's journey, data can be captured at nearly every step of the process. The challenge is keeping that data integrated across sales and marketing systems so that everyone has access to the insights needed to win.

where handoffs occur across the process will start to make the benefits of alignment seem more real, even if they have yet to be fully realized.

Knowing precisely where your data fits across find, engage, close, and grow will allow you to clearly articulate the value of data, from bringing in new opportunities to expanding your footprint within current customers.

Data's Role in Finding New Customers

At the most basic level, data helps marketing bring in new prospects by helping them determine who to target. They might use data to evaluate the current customer base and then determine attributes of the most profitable customers or those with the highest satisfaction rates. From there, marketing can build an ideal model customer or they can go deeper and look at the roles involved and develop specific targetable personas.

Having complete and accurate data helps marketing follow through on their targeting, ensuring that the right people receive the right messaging. It also helps marketing target more precisely, incorporating granular attributes like tighter revenue ranges, distinct sub-industries, or specific geographic regions. Targeting the right people with the right message leads to faster engagement and better lead qualification.

Data then helps sales close deals faster by letting them focus on more qualified leads and contacting the right person the first time. Every good sales leader knows time kills deals and speeding up flow is critical. Good data increases sales productivity by eliminating research time and dead-end leads. Data can also help increase revenues by speeding more deals through the cycle, highlighting opportunities for up-sells and cross-sells, and signaling compelling events that tip the negotiations in your favor.

Clicking down into process, data is critical not only to defining your lead-scoring model (you can only score leads on data you have) but also to ensuring leads are properly scored and correctly routed. You can think of a hundred more examples and they all require accurate *and* current data to work well.

Now you're starting to see the importance of data and the increasing importance of *good* data.

Data's Role in Engaging Customers

If you got an email right now that said, "Buy our stuff," you'd probably ignore it (if it even got past your spam filters). But if your phone buzzed right now and a message popped up that said, "Hey, I know you're reading a book about sales and marketing alignment right now," you'd probably be a bit more intrigued.

If you know little about your targets, it's difficult to effectively communicate. More accurate and current data helps you better engage with customers. It lets you predict what they need, when they need it, and why they need it, which all helps you craft a compelling pitch.

One of the things we laugh about is when a vendor gets a meeting with us and their first question is, "So, tell me about your business." Really? *You* should be telling me about my business, and why *you're* here, and how *you* can help me. That is zero engagement or it's just plain lazy.

Data helps marketing develop better personas so that broad corporate messaging can be tightened for specific roles. Targeting the manufacturing industry helps you create vaguely compelling messages. Targeting operations managers of production facilities in the manufacturing industry lets you define the message to the common pain points people in these roles are experiencing. That increases your ability to get their attention and engage quickly and effectively.

Going deeper, you'll need great data if you're thinking about account-based sales and marketing. For that, instead of targeting operations managers, you're targeting Sally, the operations manager of the Pittsburgh manufacturing plant of Westinghouse Electric. If all you had was a first name and an email address, you wouldn't even consider account-based sales and marketing.

Jon Miller is CEO and co-founder of Engagio; he was also a co-founder of Marketo. Engagio develops an account-based marketing automation solution to engage target accounts and deepen sales and marketing alignment. Jon is both an expert and a pioneer in using data to help companies better understand, engage with, and close their target accounts.

"How successful you can be with engagement really comes down to the level of account research and the level of account personalization you can do based on the quality and thoroughness of your data," Jon said on a recent InsideView webinar. "Industry-specific content is one thing. Then, maybe you're putting the prospect's logo on the cover and changing out the first and last paragraphs, which is better but still not really personalization. You need to get to the level of personalization that resonates with the recipients themselves based on what they're experiencing today."

Engagement means crafting a marketing message or a sales pitch that resonates with the customer because it's relevant and timely. Without good data, you have no idea what is relevant or timely, so engagement suffers. Ultimately, good data helps you get through all the noise being created today.

Data's Role in Closing Customers

Once you've leveraged your great sales and marketing data to get a prospect through to the opportunity phase, data becomes even more critical to closing the deal. Your data—from who is connected to whom to the latest news on an opportunity's executives—holds the secrets to precisely defining how your offering impacts the customer's business.

Data tells sales which executives to target, where future opportunities might lie, where up-sell opportunities might appear, when to cross-sell (and when to wait), and so much more. It helps the sales team craft their strategy and inform their decisions on which path to take.

Jon adds that account-based personalization is the key to closing more deals, and that takes data. "There's a classic sales tactic to find out three things about an account that are relevant and then just make sure every time you're sending them something you're using that personalization touch. That's just a start. At every stage of the deal you need to know what's relevant and what's impactful. You need to have the data, and you need to know how, when, and where to use it to go beyond engagement and through to closing the customer."

Data is power, and the more data you have over your competitors, the more power you have to win a deal.

Data's Role in Growing Customers

Data's value doesn't stop once a customer signs on the dotted line and neither does your commitment for collecting, monitoring, and maintaining it.

B2B buyers today, more and more, want a relationship with their vendors. As we mentioned earlier, more and more vendors are moving toward subscriptions and recurring revenue streams. We all know it's cheaper and easier to keep a customer than find a new one. In fact, in our experience, we've seen close rates for new opportunities within the existing customer base to have win rates twice that of brand-new prospects.

The data you have and continue to collect on your existing customers is just as important as the data you have on new prospects and leads still in the sales cycle. It can help marketing develop content and assets for better cross-selling or help sales navigate through an organization, get warm referrals to other groups, and leverage your customer for a reference for your prospective customers.

Customer data also keeps you aware of who has changed roles or left a company, which might impact renewals and deal expansions. Customers are acquired, acquire others, expand or contract their operations, enter new markets, and expand their offerings. If you have managed the relationship after the initial opportunity and your contact leaves the company, staying in touch can lead to a new opportunity with that person's new company. These are all potential opportunities for you, so you need to keep your data, insights, and connections current.

Earlier, we compared data to a river because of how it's constantly changing. A great example of this is customer satisfaction, which is like a snapshot in time. The person who claims to be satisfied may get fired tomorrow, leaving you to prove your value to someone totally unfamiliar with your offerings. Or, maybe everything has been great for years and then your product fails. A customer who was your biggest promoter yesterday may be the biggest thorn in your side tomorrow.

The point is data's importance and value doesn't end when you win a deal. You never know when a faint business signal could turn into a huge growth opportunity with an existing customer.

Data Is the Great Equalizer

Data must be the foundation for sales and marketing alignment because it is so incredibly valuable to both teams, and it's the one thing that both teams can rally around and find common value in.

Data can help you be better at sales and marketing. Good data can make you nearly unstoppable. Data is obviously critical to metrics. Everything from planning to forecasting to lead scoring depends on data. If you don't trust your data, you and your teams won't trust the metrics.

We'll also be making the case—again—that pipeline must be the common metric on which all marketing efforts are measured, and we'll make the almost radical suggestion that marketing should be *compensated* on pipeline metrics, not just leads.

Data is also critical to measuring performance and building alignment. If your data isn't clean and healthy, marketing will resist even more than expected at having their compensation tied to a totally new metric that is measured with data they don't trust.

Data is the great equalizer. This is why your alignment initiative has to include the data. Data lets you get away from opinions and feelings to focus on facts. When sales and marketing are in alignment, when your data is in alignment, there is a single source of truth on which both teams can agree. Using data as the common language fosters collaboration and improves communication.

In the end, it all comes back to growth. Good data helps both sales and marketing better target, engage, close, and grow customers, and that leads to growth.

If You Do Nothing Else About Data, Do These Things

Assuming that you've mapped all of your data sources and have clearly defined—with both sales and marketing—what creates a lead, here are your next steps:

1. Determine if all of your data is being consolidated into a single database at some point. If there is disconnected data, find out why and decide if it needs to be ignored, integrated, or turned off.

2. If you're targeting a specific market, understand the parameters of that addressable market and determine if your data includes your entire addressable market. This means all accounts, contacts, and leads based on your target personas.

3. Start the process of cleaning your data. Get some expert help, get them to gauge the state of your data cleanliness, and set up a cleaning. Be sure to look at both cleanliness and effectiveness metrics before and after the cleaning.

4. Set up a periodic cleaning and stick to it. We recommend quarterly.

5. Evaluate your data completeness and consider enrichment. Determine how many contacts in your database are missing key elements, like email address, phone number, industry, or revenue.

Push Alignment Beyond Sales and Marketing and into the CIO's Office

You've undoubtedly seen the increase in sales and marketing technology over the past several years. What began as simple email marketing tools and sales-force automation has exploded into thousands of software solutions that claim to do everything from schedule sales meetings to predict which leads are ready to buy and when.

Looking at only marketing technology, Scott Brinker, who writes the Chief Marketing Technologist blog, found 3,874 marketing technology solutions for his "2016 Marketing Technology Landscape Supergraphic." It's really overwhelming, and it's become more so over time. As technology advances in general—from Siri to self-driving cars—new and creative technologies will continue to become available for sales and marketing teams.

As a sales or marketing leader, especially one driven by alignment, all of this new technology creates a lot of background noise that must be tuned out most of the time. Eventually, however, it's part of the alignment puzzle that will need to be addressed. Luckily, we've got ideas and recommendations to help you sort it all out.

Technology Is Shifting Faster than You

What we're seeing with respect to technology is that responsibilities are shifting, new roles are being created, executives are expected to know more, and the traditional role of IT is changing. Much of the thinking around technology and the supporting cast of roles didn't even exist a decade ago. It wasn't needed, and technology was viewed from a different perspective—that of a central IT department who pushed everyone to big, company-wide enterprise resource planning (ERP) and customer relationship management (CRM) systems. Now, when it comes to technology, roles like *sales operations* and *marketing technologist* are calling the shots for their respective teams.

What do you really need to worry about? First, technology is as much a cause of misalignment as it is a facilitator of alignment. Be careful. Second, if you have a strong IT team who is agile and business focused, get them involved, leverage their technology expertise, use their overview of your company-wide technology systems. But if your organization's IT department isn't strategic or available, move forward without them.

Here are some other things to think about.

Your Technology Is out of Control

From a technology standpoint, sales uses CRM and marketing relies on marketing automation. In most cases, those two systems talk to each other and share data. If Marketo records that a prospect visited your website three times within 10 days, it can automatically change the prospect to a lead in Salesforce. That's how it's supposed to work, but now there's also social media management, predictive lead scoring, content management, and so on.

What makes it difficult is that these newer tools are cloud-based, take little to implement, and are rarely integrated with your CRM or marketing automation tools. Apps that let sales reps send email campaigns work with their Gmail accounts and never touch your

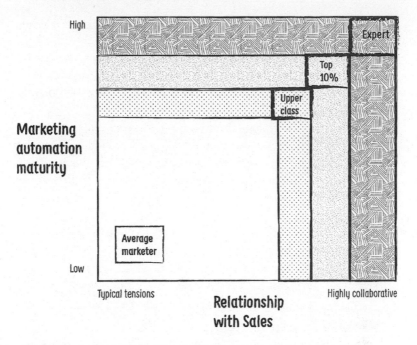

FIGURE 6.1 Forrester Research believes it takes both marketing automation maturity and a collaborative relationship with sales to improve marketing's overall impact.

Source: Forrester Research, Inc., "From Priming The Pipeline To Engaging Buyers: The B2B CMO's New Role In Sales Enablement," March, 2015

CRM systems. It takes mere minutes to write a blog post, share it on LinkedIn and Facebook, and engage and communicate with prospects far removed from any internal database. It's created a secondary layer of data that rarely, if ever, makes it into your systems of record. Furthermore, as you can see in Figure 6.1, it takes both collaboration with sales *and* technology adeptness to improve marketing's impact. Just jamming in more apps isn't the solution.

At InsideView, we recently audited our marketing technology and found software that no one used; no one knew who bought it and no one knew why we had it! We cut the cost of our marketing software by *half* in the process, and we also reduced the potential for data to leak through or stick inside individual systems. It is about more than the hard dollar costs; it is also about the cost of the distraction. Don't underestimate either. We know we're not the only ones experiencing these issues with technology.

Jason Seeba is the chief marketing technologist at BloomReach, a developer of big data marketing solutions that give customers a more relevant web experience. When he began in his role at BloomReach, he went through the same process.

"Marketing technologies should be in place to support business change," Jason says. "But there's only so much technology you can handle. With each cool new piece of software, you have to ask if you have the people who can make it work and more importantly, do you have room for it. You can't just follow the hot new software trends and get everything that comes out."

With that in mind, Jason and team combed through their marketing stack and eliminated approximately half of it. "We're now down to 6 or 10 pieces of technology, total, and it's much more manageable," Jason added. "We're also finally using it all!"

Your Data Doesn't Agree

What frequently happens in B2B companies is that marketing relies on marketing automation as their single source of truth and sales does the same with CRM. Sometimes the data doesn't agree and that causes problems.

Let's be clear: More data isn't nirvana. Garbage data produces garbage results. If you're a marketer old enough to remember renting email lists, you recall a huge percentage of those emails were stale, which is a fancy way of saying incorrect. Whether a contact was already in your system or not, stale data made them appear as a *different* contact. So while the prospect of tens of thousands of email addresses for a few hundred bucks was nice, the results were usually weak because the data was bad.

Now, we rarely rent lists, but the problem of stale data continues as contacts get promoted, quit, or move to different locations. Companies get acquired, change names, increase revenues, hire more people, or go out of business. It's a trickle, but it quickly adds up and starts to contribute to errors in decision-making, forecasting, or lead qualification, especially if sales and marketing are relying on different sets of data that don't always agree.

This combination of exploding technology and reliance on data is, like customer-centricity, both a challenge to and an opportunity for sales and marketing alignment.

View Technology as a Tool, Not a Silver Bullet

Remember that data supports alignment. Your data strategy is absolutely the backbone of your alignment initiative. Data should permeate every part of alignment, from process to people to leadership to technology; it is always the key. Technology should be acquired to support your data strategy. It is only the facilitator.

We refer to all of our sales and marketing technology as our *tech stack*. That's an old industry term related to the stacked, layer-cake–like models that software companies and IT departments use to show how all of their software components, from databases to websites to email systems, all work together (Figure 6.2). We'll use that terminology here when we refer to all of our combined sales and marketing technology.

Technology Should Support Your Data Strategy

Your tech stack should facilitate your data strategy, as we discussed in Chapter 5. You need a single source of truth, and that means agreeing on which system houses your best data. You've probably built up a lot of data silos, so now is the time to start finding them, determining the value of each, and figuring out what to do with them. Once you've pulled your sales and marketing data together, you have to maintain it. That means diagnosing the current accuracy and completeness, cleaning it regularly, and supplementing it when something is missing.

If you think that this is as simple as making a mental list of your current systems and de-duplicating it the next time you're in one of

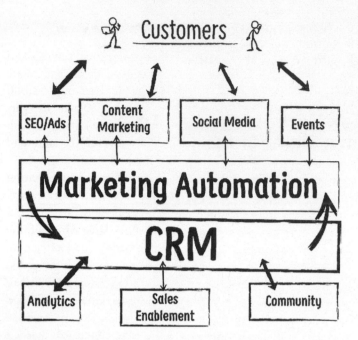

FIGURE 6.2   A typical sales and marketing technology stack, showing the customer-facing software, the core marketing automation and CRM systems, and the back-end analytics and enablement tools.

the tools, you are wrong. Creating your data strategy means sales and marketing are working together to define what you need, determine what you have, and decide how to move forward. It's not trivial and it is critical to your alignment success.

Assuming your data strategy is in place, now is the time to determine what technology is required to facilitate it. It also means killing the technology that isn't critical. That second part is interesting. In talking with many sales and marketing operations people across industries, we've found a consistent pattern: most alignment initiatives begin when someone—sales or marketing—starts investigating the root cause of bad data. In many cases, the teams eventually decide to *reduce* the size of their tech stack because too many pieces of software cause too much noise.

Do It Right: Leverage IT's Overview

JLL, formerly Jones Lang LaSalle, is a professional services and investment management company specializing in real estate and it is also an InsideView customer. They have over 58,000 employees, many of whom joined via JLL's 60-plus mergers and acquisitions over the past decade. As you can imagine, each new organization brought with it a new set of sales and marketing software.

Chad Lindsey is JLL's vice president of global information technology. He spoke at a recent InsideView customer advisory board meeting and talked about the challenges his team has had in integrating all of their customer data. Most of the challenges JLL faces, in fact, are data-related, Chad explained, and a common complaint that they hear is that IT is never fast enough. Considering the magnitude of the effort required to constantly integrate new data and new tools, Chad emphasized that it's important to take your time and stick to your strategy.

A key part of Chad's strategy was to collaboratively select a system based on what his sales and marketing teams needed, to define why that was the best decision, and to move everyone to it. As more organizations were brought into the fold, Chad was able to explain the reasoning to them and even show them the value of the selected tool. All along the way, having clean, accurate, current customer data to help their brokers engage with customers and close more deals was their primary goal.

Keep Your Eye on Alignment

As you work on your own tech stack to support your data, you'll find areas of technology that can help or hinder your alignment initiative.

One theme we keep coming back to is that collaboration is a key component of alignment. Luckily, a plethora of collaboration tools exist to cover everything from web meetings to sales content portals. With many sales reps positioned in the field, the use of web meetings and video chats is becoming more commonplace as a means of visually connecting to build internal relationships. Content portals help sales and marketing ensure that the latest versions of sales tools are always easy to find. This prevents people from being driven crazy by the futility of searching cloud storage and network drives for the latest piece of collateral.

Content is a great item to drill down into. When we say content, we mean sales and marketing content ranging from presentations, product collateral, data sheets, and campaign email templates to webinar recordings, competitive comparisons, and call scripts. Content is everything sales and marketing create to help drive engagement with customers.

Being Content with Your Content Management

Content can become one of your greatest points of alignment. It is generally created by marketing and consumed by sales, putting it at the center of a handoff point. This makes it a common area of conflict because sales often doesn't feel they have what they need and marketing can't work fast enough to create more content.

Building a process around content brings the two teams together to do exactly what we've been saying: jointly define what you want, jointly determine how it's going to happen, and jointly decide on the metrics used to measure success. Content becomes a great opportunity that forces alignment to take place. Without marketing's content, it's harder to sell. Without sales' insights, it's harder to create effective content. Sales wants good content to better engage, and marketing doesn't want to waste time creating content that's never used.

Now, back to technology. As your content library expands, sales will have a more difficult time locating the correct content. The common solution is for sales to email their favorite marketing person, who then has to find the content and email it back to the rep. As you can imagine, that is not an efficient or scalable solution.

Content management portals are becoming more popular, and even the big analyst firms are writing more about them. In a nutshell, they provide an online library for your sales and marketing content. Marketing controls what's there and sales always knows that they're getting the latest version. The reason the content management market is expanding is that frustration finding what we need is something most of us experience almost daily. A content management portal also gives marketing data on what's being used, by whom, how frequently, for which opportunities, and what was the final result. It can help them work with sales to create new content or determine which content isn't really needed.

We both agree that sales reps are constantly complaining that they can't find the content. If you have a good content management system, you're equipped to dole out some tough love in those situations because the content is always where it's supposed to be.

Do It Right: Give Sales the Right Content and Incent Them to Close the Loop

Robin Saitz is the CMO at Brainshark, which provides sales enablement solutions. Robin puts a high value on marketing content, especially as it relates to alignment.

"I see content as almost a proxy for the conversations sales reps are having with prospects. We have to make sure they have the content they need, when they need it, even before they need it. And it has to cover all the way through the on-boarding process so they can have a high-value conversation with prospects," Robin says.

Ensuring prospects see value in every conversation is marketing's responsibility, Robin says, and it's marketing's role to not only provide the content, but also to help the seller use it.

"Research says that most executives see only 20 percent of conversations with sellers as effective," Robin continues. "We have to prepare the sellers to have good conversations with the buyers, and that means we really need to understand the buyer's problems, be great on discovery, and deliver content that supports the buyer's needs."

"Misalignment happens when sales doesn't know what content is available or where it is, or when they have not been trained on how to use it in the first place. [This misalignment] turns into finger pointing, but that misses the point of whether the content even resonates with the buyer."

(Continued)

(Continued)

Through it all, Robin believes that it's still marketing's responsibility to give sales what they need to be successful, and that means much more than just a folder of content. It also means that sales has to contribute to marketing's success.

"We started with the perspective that marketing serves sales," Robin added. "I would also point out that sales owes marketing. We need them to close the loop, put their hands on the keyboard, and enter (into CRM) the disposition of the leads so we know how they're doing. They need to provide feedback and live up to the service-level agreements we have with them. That's where we need to be, so even when we get negative feedback, it's all in the spirit of advancing our company goals. Sometimes sales forgets that they have an obligation to close the loop."

Look Over There!

We'll admit that we like to geek out over new technology. We're in the middle of the tech world in San Francisco, so we hear about all of these new, cool solutions popping up, all promising to make some part of our jobs easier or faster or better. But if you let the latest shiny new object continue to distract you, you'll lose your focus on the basics of alignment. Resist the urge.

Remember data? Well, if your data isn't clean or accurate, then that fancy new predictive analytics tool isn't going to give you very accurate insights. And, if you're processes aren't well defined, if marketing can't get good data, or if sales doesn't use it, then that fancy new gizmo isn't going to help.

Resistance is not always futile. Having *intelligent resistance* means not changing for change's sake. Be discriminating and be smart. Know how to technically evaluate new tools at a high level. Understand how they will work with the other tools you already have and what value they will bring, then ask yourself if the providers will still be around in a year.

In essence, don't get distracted. Technology is not a shortcut to success. There are just way too many new offerings to even try to keep up. As you become more aligned and more advanced, then start to branch out and explore new options.

Getting on Board the Technology Train

Let's address the elephant in the room: Not everyone is *tech positive*.

We work in the technology industry and we're surrounded by colleagues and friends who are eager to use and learn new things, but we understand that the vast majority of workers are resistant to change, especially around technology. You may have rolled out the best project management tool, but there will be some people who won't use it. It's a tough situation to manage, but we feel that technology is what will, more and more often, separate the leaders from the laggards.

Now is the time to start making tough choices about how your teams move forward and who goes with them. Should someone be fired for continuing to use email to ask for content even after everyone else has moved to your new content portal? Maybe.

If some members of your teams resist new technology to the detriment of your company's growth or progress, it might be time to counsel them to start sending out their resumes to find a place that would be a better fit.

There's also a digital divide growing between sales and marketing that can hinder alignment if it's not addressed. Nancy Nardin, founder of Smart Selling Tools and an expert with over 20 years of experience in sales technology and services, has seen how marketing has jumped on the technology bandwagon while sales is just now starting to view technology as a growth driver.

"CRM has been around for 30 years, so you'd think sales would be savvier, but it's marketing who's ahead," Nancy says. "Marketing has a budget for generating leads, so dollars shift to digital spend that helps them drive leads. Marketing had to get savvy fairly quickly and they have. Marketing has money, so they can spend and experiment with new tools. Sales doesn't always have the budget or the staff.

"I see more budget in the future going toward making the rep's job easier," she added. "The overall revenue-generation process is a productivity issue. As companies look strategically at the entire process, like with alignment, you'll see it driving adoption of more tools dedicated at helping sales increase productivity. Reps can handle only so many leads so something has to be automated, like prioritizing leads based on trigger events. You need to remove friction because that's what slows the process. It's a conveyor belt. Marketing is moving leads through the process. Sales has to have the parts to pull together a deal. Friction slows everything down but technology can eliminate the friction."

Building an Alignment-Optimized Tech Stack

Alignment is driven by you, the leader, but technology can be one of your greatest enablers. Here are five areas of technology that must be part of your alignment efforts:

1. Collaboration
2. Data cleansing
3. Sales enablement
4. Dashboards and reporting
5. Predictive technologies

Collaboration

We discussed above the importance of collaboration tools with respect to communication and getting work done. It's important to standardize on one tool so that, for example, sales isn't using Slack for messaging while marketing uses Hipchat. You can't expect both teams to use *two* messaging tools, but you *can* expect one team to complain when their current technology is dropped.

Collaboration is important in alignment and improving it will help speed the process. If you can agree more quickly on your lead-scoring model, for example, then you can start working to define a

What do you think are the BIGGEST
challenges in aligning Sales and Marketing?

39% Say lack of accurate
data on target accounts!

FIGURE 6.3 Lack of accurate data on target accounts is one of the biggest challenges to sales and marketing alignment. Despite the large volumes of data available and the focus on data overall, critical insights are still missing or just plain wrong.

marketing-qualified lead. It all comes back to how well you work together, and technology can help streamline your workloads and speed your decision making.

Data Cleansing

Your sales and marketing data is currently dirty and between 2 and 5 percent of B2B company and contact data decays *per month*, according to several studies from MarketingProfs, Biznology, SiriusDecisions, and others.

Our own research found that 39 percent of sales and marketing professionals cite a lack of accurate data on target accounts as one of the biggest challenges of alignment (Figure 6.3), so it belongs at the core of your alignment efforts. You can't create alignment from inaccurate, dirty, or out-of-date data.

Data cleansing is like flossing your teeth. We all know that it's a good idea, but we seldom do it. Doing it once won't keep our gums healthy forever. Data cleansing must also be a recurring habit.

Sales Enablement

Sales enablement is a recent trend within B2B companies. The goal of sales enablement is to make sure every rep has the training, skills, processes, and assets to better engage with and win customers. Essentially, they provide support to scale the sales team efficiently.

Enablement via technology is becoming an increasingly bigger component of their role.

Since sales enablement sits between sales and marketing, we've seen companies have it report to marketing, to sales, and even directly to a CRO/CSO that has a unique view of the myriad handoff points between marketing and sales. In some cases, sales enablement works to alleviate the struggles of marketing to get content and leads to sales. In other cases, they look for ways to streamline how sales gets what they need to close more business.

Some have described sales enablement as a S.W.A.T. team that looks for roadblocks in the lead-to-revenue process, investigates their causes and impacts, and works to find and implement a solution. Others use sales enablement as the training and performance arm of sales operations. Still others use it as a catchall role designed to help sales sell more.

Regardless of the footprint, sales enablement is frequently responsible for finding technology solutions to whatever ails the sales process.

The Rise of the Sales Enablement Role

As the relationship between sales and marketing changes, roles and responsibilities are changing as well. One new role that we're seeing more and more is sales enablement. It's probably the most accurate job title around, since their role is enabling sales reps to execute more effectively.

Forrester Research, in their May 2015 report "Manage Your Sales Enablement Charter Or Run Into A Perfect Storm," defines sales enablement as "a strategic, ongoing process that equips all client-facing employees with the ability to consistently and systematically have a valuable conversation with the right set of customer stakeholders at each stage of the customer's problem-solving life cycle to optimize the return of investment of the selling system." That's a fancy way of saying that sales enablement gets the right people, processes, and content aligned behind the sales reps to help them sell more. Every company defines it a bit differently, but it generally sits between sales and marketing, and can report to either or neither, but virtually reports to both. It really doesn't matter as long as sales enablement is focused on getting sales what they need to drive growth.

Sales enablement helps alignment by pulling both teams together in the areas of data, process, and training. When a challenge is identified, sales enablement investigates the cause and determines where the data, process, or training needs to be improved to prevent it from happening again. They help sales work more effectively and efficiently, and help marketing prioritize based on sales' needs. It's a nexus point between the two teams and they are generally familiar with marketing at the campaign level and sales at the opportunity level. In meetings, they can potentially speak for either team.

We recommend that sales enablement employees have a sales background. That gives them extra credibility with sales and also helps them articulate the needs of sales better. Additionally, they also need to have a good understanding of marketing, what it takes to build a successful campaign, and how marketing decisions are made. Sometimes marketers just don't have the visibility to understand why sales needs something, so sales enablement can be that translator. It's a true hybrid role, but we've seen it be more effective if the person comes from a sales background.

While sales enablement might be a new position, you shouldn't dedicate your time getting there. In fact, you probably have some of the components in place, but housed under different domains, which means putting together your sales enablement function might be easier than you thought.

Dashboards and Reporting

We've mentioned the need for sales and marketing leaders to have knowledge that goes well beyond simple dashboards and reports. You need to know how your data works, where it flows from and to, and what it means. However, there will always be the need to convey information to your broader teams, other departments, and executives, through higher-level dashboards and reports.

The right dashboards also enable you to drill down into the details of the data. In a recent look at our internal campaign performance reports, it appeared as though our webinars—no matter how successful in terms of lead generation—weren't generating many sales opportunities. Stopping there, we might have made the decision to eliminate webinars. Instead, we dug deeper and started looking at *influenced* opportunities, which stem from leads who were already in our database—meaning they are generated by another campaign—but later attended a webinar during their lead-to-revenue journey. In fact, we found that webinars were hugely influential in turning leads into opportunities, so we doubled down on our webinar efforts.

With the right dashboards, you quickly identify trends, issues, and opportunities, but it takes a deeper look to really determine what's happening and what you should do about it.

Predictive Technologies

If you've shopped on Amazon, you've surely added things to your cart because you were told that "Customers who bought this also bought . . ." That's a well-known predictive technology, which is an emerging class of software helping B2B sales and marketing teams get better at focusing on the right targets at the right times.

For example, in most companies, leads get points added to their score based on activity. If they open an email, they get 10 points. If they download a brochure, they get 25 points. Once they reach 100 points, they're considered a marketing-qualified lead. But does that really mean anything? If you walk past a donut shop and look in the window, does that make you a likely customer? Sometimes it might, but that ignores the fact that other people might be simply checking out how their hair looks in the reflection.

Predictive technologies look far beyond the typical sales and marketing scores and metrics to make more informed predictions of who's ready to buy and when. To increase their accuracy, they might consider the time between a lead's activities, how much of a video he or she watched, or third-party data about news and events. It's a growing field with fascinating potential, so it's definitely something to add to your overall strategy.

Predictive technologies have just begun to make their way into B2B sales and marketing over the last few years. Even we are still trying to figure out where it belongs and how it can help. One thing we know for sure is that the predictions are only as good as the underlying data. That's why this is the last item on our list, not the first. Get all of your other technology ducks in a row before you start heading down this path. If not, we predict that your predictive efforts will be underwhelming.

Getting Your Budget in Order

As we've said, when sales and marketing are aligned and collude to get what they need, their jointly supported decisions and requests are tough to deny, especially by the CEO. Revenue usually trumps all else, so if you're aligned in your request for resources you *both* agree will drive revenues, you're going to get your way.

Ashu Garg, general partner at Foundation Capital, recently wrote a paper titled "MarTech and the Decade of the CMO." In it, Ashu predicts that technology spend by CMOs will increase 1,000 percent in the next 10 years, from $12 billion to $120 billion. What led him to that prediction was data showing that CMOs are on track to spend more dollars on technology than CIOs by 2017, with much of that going toward tools to help both sales and marketing predict who are the best leads, to gather as much about them as possible, and to identify the right time to engage.

While we've seen that growth in marketing spend on technology, as we're sure you have, you shouldn't expect a blank check from your CEO. But having your leadership aligned around what new pieces of technology are needed to drive revenue, efficiency, and productivity can make the CEO's decision that much easier.

Remember that Technology Should Enable, Not Detract

While we are very tech-positive, we both have to admit that we've seen tech put a drag on alignment or on sales and marketing efforts in general. In fact, we've even seen technology *cause misalignment*.

Have you ever been in a meeting representing your team and discovered that the other team had data or reports that conflicted with your findings? As we mentioned before, it happens regularly in companies without a firm data strategy, but it is also a result of their not having a handle on their technology. No matter what you say or what data you show, the other team usually leaves the meeting thinking, "They don't know what they're talking about."

It frequently happens when marketing relies on only their marketing automation system for insights and sales relies on only their CRM systems for insights. It also happens when sales and marketing add technologies without buy-in from the other team, creating an atmosphere of data ownership and information suspicion.

Where IT Fits in an Aligned Organization

Salesforce, the CRM software provider, created a $7 billion company by touting "No software" in their ads. They capitalized on the prevailing wisdom in the past 10 to 15 years that software and traditional IT infrastructure was a roadblock to getting the technology you needed to win, but now we have the hindsight to see that circumventing IT and moving to cloud-based software has added to our tech problems. It's not the software's fault. Rather it's because IT used to be the common set of eyes on every piece of software rolled out within an enterprise, but now all it takes is a credit card and a manager's approval.

Roles in sales operations, marketing operations, and sales enablement are quickly taking over the technology reins from corporate IT. And while the operations teams usually report up to their respective VP or C-level leaders, sales enablement is less defined and usually at least has a dotted-line responsibility to one or both sales and marketing executives.

There are still some potential obstacles to be aware of with these roles that could arise in situations like deploying new marketing tools without sales buy-in. If not orchestrated well, from both the data and political perspectives, they might cause more friction.

The same is true even as aligned teams work with or without IT. Our advice is to keep IT involved at least as a technical expert but probably more. IT will know the nitty-gritty technical challenges that you may not. On the one hand, if the fancy cloud-based analytics dashboard that you're in love with works only in the Chrome web browser, IT can flag potential issues, like the fact that most of the company still uses Internet Explorer. On the other hand, suppose you've narrowed down your predictive lead-scoring purchase to two options and are unsure of the technical pros and cons. Bringing IT in at the last minute can cause delays, roadblocks, resentment, and foot-dragging.

In many companies, and because of the ease of buying and implementing modern technology, IT has been eliminated from most buying decisions. More often they are tasked with looking after legacy software, managing email servers, and taking care of laptops and printers.

In some ways, this trend eliminates yet another chef in the technology kitchen, one who wasn't intimately involved in the business decisions that needed to be made. In other ways, removing IT from technology purchase decisions has exacerbated misalignment. IT was the one team with insight across all corporate technologies, databases, and integrations. They could remind marketing that sales has standardized on specific software that was incompatible with something marketing wanted.

Do It Right: Give IT a Chance to Add Value

Alvina Antar is the CIO of Zuora, a provider of relationship business management services. She's been looking at B2B businesses from the perspective of IT for nearly 20 years, and sees both the importance of IT's involvement in the overall technology structure as well as the need for IT departments to be more agile and more responsive to the needs of the business units.

"There has been a lot of talk about the CMO taking the CIO's role as the largest buyer of technology," Alvina says. "The real issue is both the CMO and CIO need to build a true

(Continued)

(Continued)

partnership, and that begins with a level of trust and confidence in each other. If the CIO can't work with the agility the business needs, of course the CMO is going to go out on his or her own. Customer-facing teams can't wait because time-to-market is key. The CMO needs to trust the technology leader so they can focus on the business of marketing. If not, he or she is spending too much time on implementations instead.

"Where the CIO can really help is integrating new tools into the bigger ecosystem. There is so much value in having visibility into what the rest of the company is doing. Similarly, CIOs also help to avoid duplication of capabilities when there are lots of tools and many overlap."

We've said you should include the IT department in technology decisions. That's where they have expertise and you don't. But, just as a modern CMO or sales VP should have a fundamental understanding of the technology, the CIO needs to have an understanding of the needs of sales and marketing from a business perspective.

"The onus is on the technology leader to understand the marketers' or sales reps' business," Alvina added. "A technology leader can't implement something unless they understand the business.

By keeping IT involved in a consultative capacity, you can reap the benefits of their knowledge without the added encumbrance of yet another potential project veto or delay. Security is a prime example. It's a major threat these days and IT is more qualified than most other executives to effectively evaluate potential risks.

Better yet, with so much riding on your sales and marketing data, it is IT's job to know how data and systems work together. We talked about the data silos that both sales and marketing have erected over the years of misalignment. With IT, those silos could have been avoided, or at least the risks would've been known ahead of time.

Be aware, however, that IT does come with some red tape, especially in larger companies. Having spent both of our careers in the software industry, we have seen again and again how IT involvement can stall and even derail software implementations. They're responsible for more than just email systems and revenue-side technology. Don't forget all of the financial, human resources, customer service, inventory, ordering, procurement, and other systems IT has to support throughout your company.

Hey IT, Up Your Game

We're going out on a bit of a limb here by advising you to keep IT involved. For some, your experiences working with IT may not be positive and you may think that keeping them involved is a recipe for disaster. So we also have some advice for IT: Start upping your game. By that, we mean they should become closer and more familiar with the actual business issues driving requests for technology. Align IT with sales and marketing for a while, understand their pain, and dig deeper into why they need a solution. It'll help to maintain IT's value as more than just the fix-it team for laptops and printers.

Do It Right: Build Trust with Your CIO

IT needs to get on board or get out of the way, in our opinion. But, obviously, getting them on board as a critical ally can both take work off of your team and create a better technology stack in the process. For aligned sales and marketing leaders, you need to build the same sort of alignment with your CIO.

"My CIO actually wants to help and he puts high priority on marketing projects," says Kim DeCarlis, who is CMO at Imperva, a provider of cyber security solutions, and also holds an engineering degree from Stanford University. "The most important way to engage him is to keep him aware of what's happening and what's coming, and bring his team into the tent early to help with business requirements, project definitions, and so on."

(Continued)

(Continued)

Just as marketing needs to get closer to the customer to better understand the challenges sales faces, both sales and marketing need to do the same with your CIO to gain their respect and trust.

"I've written code," Kim added. "I have a technical background. I came up through product marketing in software companies. I use that to establish common ground, and I was able to establish it early. But once that trust was established, we could get straight to the marketing objectives, show IT how it helps them achieve their goals, and show them what I need from them."

Once you're dealing with the business objectives, the conversation with the CIO becomes more about solving the problems and supporting growth.

"I don't want more technology," Kim says. "I don't want to be in charge of the network, the hardware, the security. I make it very clear what I want to focus on, and that's helping this company grow."

Collusion Is Such a Dirty Word, but It Works

Sales and marketing have, for years, been getting their way with IT requests, mostly because they are generating the profits that run the company. We've shown why alignment around technology makes both teams stronger, but you still might have issues selling large and expensive technology budget requests with your CEO. Remember that there's little a CEO can do to resist more revenue.

Combining requests as a joint sales and marketing budget item might be seen as another form of sales and marketing collusion, but think of it as the fruits of your alignment efforts. Combined teams with a single vision and goal are much more powerful. It also brings IT into the fold, giving them less power to resist a valid and valuable technology.

Consider Your Own Revenue-Focused IT Team

Another emerging role we've seen is director of business systems, especially in firms with weak or nonstrategic IT teams. This role focuses purely on sales and marketing technology, becoming a de facto IT department for sales and marketing. The difference here is the role requires sales and/or marketing experience and knowledge, not just technical expertise. The goal is facilitating growth through technology.

This might be seen as eliminating IT altogether, but think of it more as an in-between role that can talk intelligently to both a VP of sales and a CIO. They can also become the right hand of the sales or marketing leader, giving technology advice and educating the executives on what's new and what's necessary.

Keep Your Own Saw Sharpened

The VPs of sales and the CMOs of tomorrow may look much different from how we look today. Both will clearly need to continually stay educated on the role of technology in our domains. We'll need to stay smart on our data, where it's coming from, and what it's telling us, and we'll need to know how to analyze that data to guide our growth.

Yet again, the paths toward alignment and the future converge around new and changing skills and roles. Executives can't sit back and rely on more technically savvy employees to fill in the gaps. Executives need to know at least the basics. Just as we dinged IT for not knowing the business issues, don't be the sales or marketing executive that gets dinged for not understanding the technology.

If You Do Nothing Else About Technology, Do These Things

1. Audit all of your technology systems and create a map of your own technology stack. Know what you have, what it does, and how it's integrated. Give yourself bonus points if you do it together as sales *and* marketing.

(Continued)

(*Continued*)

2. Connect with your CIO to talk about your aligned path forward. Understand their skills and their bandwidth—and appetite—to take on more strategic projects. You might gain a new ally in your alignment initiative.

3. Review your tech stack with your team, discuss what each tool does, and decide if it's useful enough to maintain or if it's unused or providing little value. Prepare to make some go/no-go decisions about keeping some tools.

4. Identify the gaps in your tech stack and create a team to investigate solutions. If you're weak on collaboration tools, look into them. If you're advanced and think you can handle predictive tech, start doing some research.

5. Document all your vendor relationships, contracts, and renewal dates. Most of the CMOs we know have received an auto-renewal invoice only to realize that no one is using the technology but they're stuck in a contract for another year!

Chapter 7

Cracking the Code of Alignment

As we've mentioned a few times throughout this book, we conducted a detailed survey of nearly 1,000 sales and marketing professionals to uncover the real reasons behind our misalignment. Some of the findings confirmed our hunches and others really surprised us. We found miscommunication and misconceptions are the top two reasons for misalignment, but digging deeper, we found even more disconnects. Let's review our motivation for conducting this research.

Both of us have always believed sales and marketing should be talking to each other more. Once we were well into our own alignment transition, we believed *we* should be talking more *about* sales and marketing. We had our own opinions and, because Inside-View sells to both sales and marketing, they gave us the opportunity to see how the two teams interact and communicate across all different customer types, company sizes, industries, and segments. What we heard usually confirmed our assumptions, but we wanted to be sure.

Getting the sentiment of an entire market takes work, but we thought it would allow us to see the basics. It would uncover the

Alignment 101 items—communication, collaboration, and metrics—that would take us out of our echo chamber where alignment was always great and ground us with what real professionals are actually thinking and feeling. Sometimes you just have to ask some questions to gauge if what you *think* you know is really what's happening.

We've experienced firsthand the effects of misalignment, on ourselves, our teams, and our companies. We've felt the tension, been embroiled in the conflicts, and been through the pain. And we both had seen it in every job we've had. Every one!

When the two of us got together, it was the exact opposite. After a while, we started to wonder why. Were we just lucky or were there others out there who, like us, longed for an alignment-enlightened counterpart? Was alignment unique to high tech? Was it widespread? How are others dealing with it?

The only way to find out was to ask. Coincidently, InsideView's customers were the exact people we wanted to survey, since they are at the white-hot center of misalignment, so we decided to go directly to them. What we found was that our hunches were true, and that many people—both in sales and in marketing—were either living in the drag of misalignment or reveling in the benefits of alignment. Our clients' business success was correlated to their degree of alignment.

Once we completed our research and looked at the results, it was a call to action to do something more, which led to this book. We saw a clear signal that there was more to explore, more to discuss, and more to share. The stories we heard were real and revelatory, and we wanted to learn more. That's why you've read so many interviews and case examples throughout this book: because we interviewed more than 50 experts, professionals, educators, analysts, researchers, and executives to get their perspectives and help us explain how to become an aligned organization.

Uncovering the Roots of Misalignment

An adversarial relationship between sales and marketing has been the norm for decades. The root of it is we really don't know what each other does because we're focused on totally different fundamental goals: marketing generates a constant flow of many leads, while sales builds a pipeline of individual qualified opportunities.

Sales Is Deal Focused

It is crystal clear how sales is measured: attaining quota. To do that, we need to close deals. To do *that*, we need to understand customers at the granular level, which means focusing on individual accounts and opportunities. This means research, engagement, understanding connections, and much more. What are the prospect's driving pain points, their decision-making process, their past experience, their preferences, and their buying process? Who are the internal influencers and how do I engage with them? What are their unique goals, challenges, and desired outcomes? What's their timeline? What are the competing projects? Who are we competing with? Who owns the budget?

Depending on the size and scale of a deal, it quickly becomes a significant responsibility. And that's just for a single opportunity. A rep may need to close scores of deals every quarter just to make quota. So while, from the outside, sales appears to be singularly driven by quota, their job is much, much more than just sending quotes and negotiating contracts. A lot of skill and effort goes into a deal way before a quote is ever generated.

To be in sales requires a special personality with a unique attitude, because it's such a demanding role with tremendous pressure. Reps are generally impatient, persistent, and controlling—and that's intentional. That's what makes a successful salesperson. It also makes us not so good at sharing information, being patient, or being collaborative.

Marketing Is Lead Focused

Marketing's role in a company is broad, spanning across brand building, awareness, content delivery, events, and more, but it is generally *measured* on filling and pushing leads through the funnel. Generating leads is our primary goal. But in order to do that, we need to identify and understand the target markets. We need to know buyer personas and deeply understand who they are, why they buy, and where their motivations lie. We try to understand the competition, see their strengths and weaknesses, and evaluate their presence.

We also focus on productivity and efficiency, trying to squeeze more and better leads out of the resources we have. We try to build name recognition across the market, yet we also try to make each interaction feel unique and personal. When we're doing well, sales thanks us (when they're not busy closing deals). When we're not doing so well, sales blames lack of pipeline for missed quotas.

Marketers are creative and view longer-term goals over deal-specific wins. We're also becoming more and more data-driven, especially in the last 10 years as marketing automation has made it possible.

Those were our opinions. What did our survey find?

Challenges to Alignment

We opened our survey with a simple question: What do you think are the biggest challenges in aligning sales and marketing. The responses are shown in Figure 7.1.

Like many problems in life, communication is the top issue. It is cited by nearly half of sales and marketing professionals as the top reason sales and marketing are not aligned. The survey revealed that

Challenges to Alignment
What do you think are the biggest challenges in aligning Sales and Marketing?

Communication	49%
Processes are broken/flawed	42%
Measured by different metrics	40%
Lack of accurate data on target accounts	39%

FIGURE 7.1 The biggest challenges to alignment, according to our survey, are communication, broken processes, different measurements, and a lack of accurate data.

the communication breakdown has many dimensions, such as how leads are being converted and what levers might be affecting performance and close rates. That means marketers won't be able to identify where lead-quality issues may be occurring.

The second highest-ranked issue is a lack of defined and workable business processes, specifically those that tie directly to the lead funnel. Agreement on key factors, such as lead flow, what makes a qualified lead, and the process to examine the pipeline, are absent and contribute to misalignment. Pipeline is key and is arguably where the true integration between sales and marketing occurs. The lead handoff from marketing to sales is not the final step. Before a lead makes it into the pipeline, there must be an agreement on what qualifies as pipeline and how it will be measured.

Forty percent of respondents identified disconnected metrics as a challenge to sales and marketing alignment, making it the third highest-ranked challenge. Sales is typically measured on quota attainment, win rates, and renewals, yet none of those show up on marketing's radar, because marketing is traditionally only worried about leads. With both teams focused on different metrics and aspects of leads and accounts, it's no wonder there is conflict.

Closely following was lack of accurate data on target accounts. If time is wasted chasing the wrong leads or performing manual research, productivity falls and frustration grows. As noted earlier, a marketing-qualified lead is of little use to a sales rep if that lead isn't at that company any longer, or has moved departments, or doesn't have an accurate email address or phone number.

What Separates Alignment Leaders and Laggards

Leading companies—those who exceed their revenue goals—realize the path to successful alignment centers around shared priorities. Of those surveyed, a majority of respondents reported exceeding or meeting revenue goals in the last year, while 22 percent fell short. We found patterns among the leaders that reveal a more sophisticated approach to alignment. These findings can inform best practices for teams that are looking to strengthen alignment.

Leaders tend to have better processes in place and they use emerging tools such as data enrichment to fuel more effective and collaborative prospecting efforts. Overall, leaders also have far greater confidence in the quality of leads generated and they are three times more likely to characterize lead quality as "excellent" compared with laggards.

The sales and marketing executives of the leaders consistently reported better relationships with their counterparts. Additionally, while the research shows that sales and marketing teams are simply not meeting often enough, a higher percentage of sales leaders conduct weekly meetings with their marketing team.

Why the Leaders Are Leading

Alignment leaders demonstrate strength in four key areas that are foundational to alignment: communication skills, common pipeline measurement, adherence to lead quality, and data enrichment to drive successful prospecting. Let's take a look at each of these areas.

Better Communication Skills

Our survey found that sales and marketing are miles—well, months, really—apart on their impression of communication frequency. As we also noted in Chapter 1, we asked each team specifically how often they meet with the other team to discuss pipeline. Shockingly, most salespeople said it was less than quarterly while most marketers said it was weekly (Figure 7.2).

Our research showed that affinity measures (e.g., do we like each other and get along, etc.) are high between sales and marketing. Sales and marketing executives would do well to build upon that by focusing on improving communication and fostering camaraderie between the two teams.

The alignment mission and message should stem from the top down and we've mentioned many of these methods, such as having weekly reviews of marketing campaigns to promote accountability and to help you avoid blindsiding the sales team. But other things executives can do include discussing lead scoring frequently with your counterparts, examining lead routing on a regular basis to ensure it's working properly, and building relationships and a collaborative culture from the top and by example.

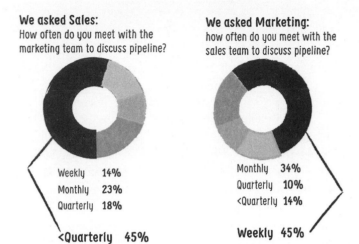

We asked Sales:
How often do you meet with the
marketing team to discuss pipeline?

Weekly   14%
Monthly   23%
Quarterly 18%

<Quarterly   45%

We asked Marketing:
how often do you meet with the
sales team to discuss pipeline?

Monthly   34%
Quarterly 10%
<Quarterly 14%

Weekly   45%

FIGURE 7.2   A question regarding how often meetings occur to discuss pipeline resulted in widely different answers from sales and marketing teams.

This PhD Says Communication Is the Key

Sharmila C. Chatterjee is a senior lecturer of marketing and academic head of the Enterprise Management Track at MIT's Sloan School of Management. She has a PhD in marketing from the Wharton School at the University of Pennsylvania and carried out some of the first studies on the interface of sales and marketing.

"Leadership on alignment has to come from the top," Sharmila says. "Leadership has to encourage and motivate their teams for alignment, but it also has to be grassroots. The people have to buy into this and take pride in it. They have to embrace alignment at the grassroots level."

To get teams motivated, Sharmila suggests increasing communication by finding pockets of success and spreading the word, but you have to choose the right people to use as your models.

(Continued)

(Continued)

"If you have a few people doing great individual work but who aren't respected, they aren't good role models," Sharmila explained. "Pick a region or territory that's working well and add resources to make it even better. Document what's happening and what works and doesn't work. Then hold them up, communicate it throughout your organization, and recognize them. Everyone wants to succeed. When others see what works and gets the attention, they will try to adopt those same things. Over time, it takes over, becoming internalized and institutionalized."

Just as you want to have hard numbers when you create customer case studies, Sharmila advocates quantifying your alignment success as well. As you communicate more about alignment, it's important to have metrics to strengthen your message around alignment's benefits.

"We can draw a parallel with value selling. Value selling is considered by several thought leaders as being critical to performance over the long term," Sharmila adds. "You can't just say something is better; you have to say why it's better and quantify it. You have to say, 'Use my product and it will increase revenue by X percent or cut costs by Y percent.' That works internally as well. Coincidently, companies that rely on value-based selling have close coordination between sales and marketing. The medical products and device industry has done this well. Sales and marketing need to collaborate and coordinate and share the information and the data that helps them prove their value."

At the tactical level, Sharmila's doctoral dissertation focused on sales leads and the black hole they seem to fall into. While marketing is quick to focus on the lack of sales follow-up, it's important to center on the lead-quality issue, which surfaces alongside many other organizational issues. If you guessed communication was one of them, you'd be right.

"Sales has time constraints," she explained. "It's not possible for them to follow up on all of the leads coming in. There has to be real coordination, an understanding of the sales cycles, and an understanding of the capacity sales has. What about whom the leads go to? Are they constrained with something else? The appropriate allocation of leads to the right person at the right time becomes critical. If sales and marketing aren't talking, that becomes a huge challenge. And tech isn't a savior here; it's human capital that has to come in and do the work."

In the end, it all comes back to communication, plain and simple, according to Sharmila. "Given today's fast-paced environment, managers may not have time to harness needed intelligence from the technology-facilitated trove of collected data," she says. "However, being informed is especially important to meet the needs of today's knowledgeable customers during their iterative purchase journey. Herein comes the role of the joint cross-functional meetings where there could be rich, relevant information sharing, which is actionable, with outcomes that are observable and thus serve as an effective feedback mechanism."

There you go: Alignment begins with a conversation. Now go talk with your colleagues!

Constant Process Review and Improvement

Ensure that you have good processes on critical alignment topics such as lead scoring and routing. These topics aren't set-it-and-forget-it items. They require regular review and examination to ensure they are working properly. Scoring should be revisited at least twice each year, if not quarterly. Lead routing should be monitored by marketing operations and sales development leaders to ensure no lead is lost or falls into the wrong hands. We all know that if a lead gets routed improperly, the recipient will just move on to the next thing—they don't often take the time to reroute. Once that happens, leads are gone forever. Marketing might as well light money on fire!

This finding is as much process as it is communication but we found that many teams don't even meet to discuss lead scoring. You've probably noticed by now that we've mentioned lead scoring

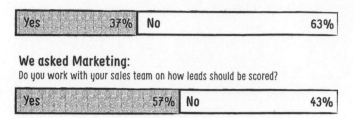

We asked Sales:
Do you meet with your marketing team on how leads should be scored?

| Yes | 37% | No | 63% |

We asked Marketing:
Do you work with your sales team on how leads should be scored?

| Yes | 57% | No | 43% |

FIGURE 7.3 Sales and marketing have differing views on how often they communicate, especially on important items, such as pipeline and lead scoring.

again and again as one of the starting points for alignment. It's a conversation starter, and it's behind the biggest handoff between sales and marketing (Figure 7.3).

Shifted Focus to Lead Quality

A focus on lead quality over quantity is critical to the successful alignment between teams; attaining high-quality leads is *de rigueur* for leaders polled in the study (Figure 7.4). The leaders had far greater confidence in lead quality than the laggards. Forty-five percent of those who exceeded revenue goals said quality was

We asked Sales:
What do you want most from marketing?

Better-quality leads

| | 55% |

More leads

| | 44% |

FIGURE 7.4 By a wide margin, more than half of sales professionals say that the number-one thing they want from marketing is better-quality leads.

"good" or "excellent," compared to only 22 percent for laggards. Conversely, among the leaders, only 15 percent characterized lead quality as "below average." That contrasts with one-third of laggards citing "below average" lead quality.

A bonus to emphasizing lead quality over lead quantity is that it encourages collaboration between sales and marketing to place definitions around a *qualified* lead. In fact, the number of leaders who reported that they meet to discuss lead scoring was more than three times greater than the number of laggards.

Better, More Complete Prospect Data

A lack of data or lack of a complete picture of targeted leads can stall the team's ability to align. It can cause problems in lead routing and follow-up.

More than half of respondents said data and lead enrichment are the most important emerging tools for driving successful prospecting. Of those who prioritized data and lead enrichment, 40 percent are leaders.

Marketers also pointed out that they are lacking data to identify the prospects most likely to convert, a challenge for 43 percent of respondents. An increasing number of marketers are tackling this challenge by working in house or with vendors to get the data needed to target more accurately.

At Least We Can All Be Friends

Andrea was at InsideView a few quarters before Tracy, and was ready for a better, more collaborative relationship with her marketing lead. Tracy had experienced the typical adversarial sales and marketing relationships as CMO in previous roles and was looking for an opportunity more rewarding than the norm. Both of us were tired of misalignment, and we wanted our careers to be sources of happiness, not stress-filled emotional drains. And we succeeded!

If you haven't already figured it out, in addition to Tracy running marketing and Andrea running sales at InsideView, we became close friends. We got along great from the moment we met during Tracy's very first round of interviews for the CMO role.

Tracy disarmed Andrea's skepticism by stating early in the conversation that marketing exists to make sales easier. Andrea built early trust with Tracy by acknowledging that sales couldn't be successful without good marketing. (It also helped that the first meeting during Tracy's interview process coincided with the company's Friday happy hour. Andrea showed up for their late-afternoon meeting with a glass of champagne!)

Now, after 18 months of working together, we've built a tight bond that enables us to outperform because we spend less time worrying about fights and blame and more time focusing on our jobs. It also makes us happier at our jobs, which makes everything that much more rewarding.

You may not be best friends with your counterparts right now, but through alignment, you will strengthen your foundation. One of the bright spots of the survey was discovering, at least on the human side, alignment isn't going to be a difficult personal slog for most sales reps and marketers (Figure 7.5).

While it does appear that marketers are a bit more attached than sales reps, the numbers point to an easy transition from barely

We asked Sales:
How would you describe your
relationship with your marketing team?

 Excellent or Good **58%**

We asked Marketing:
How would you describe your
relationship with your sales team?

 Excellent or Good **77%**

FIGURE 7.5   At least most of us in sales and marketing like each other.

meeting, to meeting much more frequently, to maybe even having a
nice lunch with each other!

If You Do Nothing Else About Understanding Your Misalignment, Do These Things

1. Survey your teams to uncover areas of mistrust, confusion, and frustration. Tools like SurveyMonkey and Google Forms allow you to create simple surveys with anonymous results. It's a quick way to take the pulse of larger teams or to encourage more timid people to give honest answers without being in a public spotlight during a meeting.

2. Start meeting more frequently to specifically discuss pipeline, lead quality, and process issues. Call out the topic in the name of the meeting so there is no confusion and create an agenda that provides a forum for honest feedback and an exchange of ideas. Be proactive to avoid finger-pointing and blame if it crops up.

3. Drive the message throughout the teams. It's not enough to meet at the leadership level. Every member of the sales and marketing team should understand the goals, measures, and challenges.

4. Bat from each other's corner. Seek out reasons to see an issue from the others' point of view and advocate for something that will help make their life easier.

5. Get to know your colleagues on a personal level. Seek to understand their joys and interests and what makes them tick. Start more conversations with "What are you doing this weekend?" instead of "What's up with all of those crap leads?"

Leading-Edge Concepts for Reaching Complete Alignment

You've now read our thoughts on alignment, our ideas for how to align, and what dozens of analysts, thought leaders, and executives had to say about the benefits of alignment. Now what are you going to do about it?

It may seem overwhelming today, but think about how alignment is going to make your job so much more satisfying—and fun! It'll be more rewarding and you'll feel more trust, especially on a personal level. When there is trust, there can be experimentation. You'll want to try new things and stretch beyond the status quo. We both love coming to work but that wasn't always the case. The biggest source of stress for sales and marketing employees is each other. Alignment (nearly) eliminates that stress.

When we started thinking about this book, we split the journey to alignment into four key sections: leadership, culture, process, and technology. Even if you're starting from a place of *slight* alignment, your move to full alignment isn't going to be a tiptoe through the proverbial tulips.

When you think about your immediate future and how you're going to begin, realize that this is going to be difficult at some points and seemingly impossible at others. We want to prepare you to stretch outside of your comfort zone, to step beyond the boundaries of what you know, and what you're currently responsible for. We want to show you where you might step on some toes. The most important thing is to never forget that your eventual future is bright. With that in mind, let's walk through your immediate objectives and what the long-term future holds for sales, marketing, and the path to alignment.

Prepare for What's Next

When we think about being prepared to react, we're reminded of a presentation by SiriusDecisions' service director, Mark Levinson, and their VP and group director, Jay Gaines. The report was titled "The Revenue Ecosystem: Aligning Sales, Marketing and Product to Outperform." In their discussion, they brought up a significant problem with alignment: "It breaks all the time!"

The SiriusDecisions team went on to list examples of things that can disrupt your alignment success. Maybe a competitor launches a new offering. Maybe your field sales team underperforms. Maybe you're going to miss your quarterly targets. When those types of things happen, alignment initiatives can take a back seat as sales focuses completely on closing deals, to the exclusion of all else. If marketing maintains the status quo of lead quality and quantity instead of picking up the slack, that can also undermine alignment.

Their point is that *stuff* happens, so you need to be prepared. Better yet, you need to be vigilant at all times, watching the market, monitoring competitors, talking with customers and analysts. When something goes wrong, sales will most likely have to focus on closing deals, so it's marketing's responsibility to keep their eyes open and crank up their performance.

By this point we're confident you've bought off on the concept and importance of alignment and how it can help your company

7 predictions for the future of alignment

1. The rise of the consultative seller
2. Millennials have a major impact
3. Cross-training becomes imperative
4. Academia catches up
5. Marketing compensation gets tied to pipeline
6. Account-based everything is a top priority
7. Customer data strategy rises in importance

FIGURE 8.1   Our predictions for the future of alignment.

grow. But, as with all great concepts, even when you do reach alignment, you can't just sit on it. Keeping your alignment edge means constantly preparing for and evaluating what's coming next.

Here are our predictions on what the future of alignment holds (Figure 8.1).

Prediction #1—The Rise of the Consultative Seller

We discussed the changing role of both sales and marketing, and specifically the drastic changes expected for B2B sales in the near future. It's going to quickly force you to rethink how leadership, culture, process, and technology all work together with these evolving roles to drive alignment.

As we have discussed often in this book, the concept of B2B sales is rapidly evolving. This evolution will affect your company culture, your leadership styles and tactics, and the processes you currently have in place. Mary Shea at Forrester Research authored a report titled "The B2B Sales Force Digital Reboot." In it, Mary talks about the four seller archetypes currently found in B2B companies: order takers, explainers, navigators, and consultants. Order takers do just that and are suited for low-complexity offerings. Explainers focus on the product. Navigators use relationships to win where buyers have complex politics or processes.

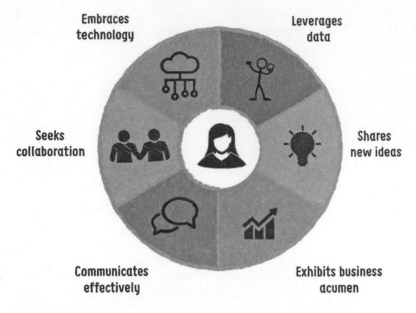

FIGURE 8.2 Forrester Research's Mary Shea points to these characteristics of consultant sellers as what will help them thrive in the changing buyer landscape.

Source: Forrester Research, Inc., "The B2B Sales Force Digital Reboot," October, 2015

The number of B2B salespeople fitting those three archetypes, according to Mary, will decline drastically by 2020. The B2B salesperson of the future will instead fill a consultative role and use quantitative analytical skills, technology, and data savvy; have financial and operation knowledge; and be able to engage with everyone from the c-suite to attorneys to procurement managers (Figure 8.2).

We're seeing this evolution happening already in the tech industry, as demonstrated by the explosion of cloud-based products that need *no* salespeople, but it's time to start thinking about how it's going to impact your industry and your business. Buyers are doing more of the work themselves, so the traditional sales model is changing quickly.

With it, the marketing model will change also. Sales will need different types of content created from different perspectives. We're already seeing content marketing take more resources, with how-to articles and the free flow of ideas and solutions creating more engagement over direct pitches. Marketing will move from branding and messaging to data and analytics.

Marketing continues to get more budget, more technology, and more power, so what's next? We see some industries rolling the evolving sales role under marketing and redefining sellers who act as hybrids of sales and marketing. They'll be experts on the industry, the buying personas, and the products, as good marketers should be. But they'll also be experts at adapting to each buyer's journey, and their unique needs and internal politics. There will be less negotiating and more partnering.

Prediction #2—Millennials Have a Major Impact

In 2016 Millennials surpassed Baby Boomers as the nation's largest living generation, according to the U.S. Census Bureau. Whether you're prepared or not, they are entering the workforce, shaping how companies are created, and changing the expectations of what work is.

Millennials are more team oriented, more tech savvy, and less bound by traditional thinking. As employees, they have different expectations on education, communication, and career advancement. As leaders, they will use those expectations to change how businesses work. Start thinking about how you're going to adapt to their ways of working, not how you're going to get them to adapt to yours.

In the Forrester report co-authored by Mary Shea, "May The Force Of The Millennials Be With You!," which we referenced earlier, Forrester offers a few recommendations for "putting in place the right building blocks to enlist and engage this exciting group of current and future revenue generators." In summary, they suggest the following:

- Making training and procedures more relevant, interesting, and engaging to Millennials.

- Mentoring them continuously to guide them to the next steps in their careers and mentoring in reverse so you can learn new things from them.

- Positioning management to be more flexible to the needs of Millennials and the dynamics and sensitivities associated with this generation.

Something else to always keep in mind, whether you're bringing on a new Millennial right out of school or you're recruiting a seasoned Boomer as a top executive, is to hire for alignment. If you hire a CMO who's only interested in generating leads and building brand, that CMO might not be interested in helping sales win more deals. Similarly, hiring an inside sales rep who views marketing as subservient is just as disruptive.

While there is no litmus test for alignment readiness, here are a few interview questions that might help you determine if a candidate is ready for alignment.

- Describe a healthy relationship between sales and marketing.
- Give me an example of a break in communication or process that you had with your counterpart (in sales or marketing) and how you found a solution.
- Tell me about the interaction or handoff points between sales and marketing in your previous companies.
- Tell me about the executive relationships you've seen between sales and marketing and how that impacted the teams.
- How would you measure marketing's impact on sales?

Prediction #3—Cross-Training Becomes Imperative

The best way to learn is to do. You get a better restaurant manager if that person has also cooked and been on the waitstaff. An experienced manager also gets more respect from the teams in the trenches. The same works for sales and marketing.

Sales leaders are always offering to have marketers attend sales calls, and marketers are always inviting sales reps to marketing meetings. That's not enough. It has to be a job requirement; even going so far as to have an exchange program is a great idea. Incentivize people to spend a month or a quarter working within the other team.

Younger workers are more open to the concept of cross-training. Older workers like us were taught to choose a career path and stick with it, but that is not the case with Millennials. They are inherently more flexible. They seek out experiences outside of their domains more readily than past generations.

Have marketers make cold calls or customer-satisfaction survey calls one day per quarter. Put sales reps on event planning teams and require them to do more than just staff the booth. Add a goal to each marketer's objectives to attend five field sales meetings per quarter. They should be doing these things already, but when they aren't required, they get overlooked or pushed aside. Progressive companies are putting these types of activities into the goals and objectives of sales and marketing teams.

Tracy had the chance to convene and host a select panel of experts at a recent MarTech conference. Her final question to panelists asked what their advice would be to their 25-year-old selves. Kim DeCarlis, CMO at Imperva, whose thoughts on marketing technology were shared in Chapter 6, had three simple suggestions for marketers. One was to accept lateral career moves to build skills and experience. Another was to volunteer for international assignments. But her number-one piece of advice was this: "Take a customer-facing, revenue-producing role as early as you can. When you join marketing, that experience will give you untold credibility with sales."

While having marketing experience is not as relevant for sales, even Andrea mentioned earlier in this book how her experience on a marketing events team helped widen her view of what goes into marketing campaigns and programs. No matter your role, having spent time in the shoes of the other is invaluable.

Sales shouldn't wait to be asked, however; they should be pulling marketing into their business, according to Tracy Birdsall, vice president and head of sales for enterprise, global ePayments, and fraud management at Visa, the global payments company. "Sales should bring marketing into more meetings," she says. "Sales has to pull them out from behind their desks. How will feedback ever get back to marketing? For sales, part of their role is to get feedback from the customer. It's to tell marketing how their value proposition is resonating with customers. Marketing rarely hears that message being delivered nor how it's received by the customer.

"When marketing is there, hearing it for themselves, it removes the friction of sales giving marketing bad news about how their message fell flat," she adds.

It's that firsthand experience that not only removes the friction of not-so-great news, but also builds trust when you see what the other team hears, understand what they're going through, and realize that they aren't always exaggerating or complaining. You only get that by being there in person.

Forrester Research Says Sales and Marketing Will Change Drastically in Just the Next Few Years

Peter O'Neill is a vice president and research director at Forrester Research, where he is focused on trends in B2B marketing and sales enablement. We asked for his predictions on the future of sales and marketing. Here's what he had to say.

What's happening to B2B sales and marketing?

Consumer businesses invest about 10 times more in marketing than they do in sales. In B2B, it's the opposite, with sales getting about 10 times more investment than marketing. In 2015 we released a report, "Death Of A (B2B) Salesman," stating that one million B2B salespeople in the United States will lose their jobs to self-service e-commerce by 2020. It's not as simple as that, but I think we will see B2B companies move toward a 50-50 split in their investments in sales and marketing, so marketing continues to become more important, and that's going to be over just the next four years.

The report you mention also states that marketing is getting more involved in the entire customer life cycle. What will marketing do differently?

Marketing will be more active with content marketing, with leadership efforts in the discovery and exploration phases of the customer life cycle. Marketing will also get more active in the buying phase and in the user experience, onboarding, and post-deal advocate marketing.

There are issues with the handoff points. Right before the customer signs a contract, there is a lot of engagement. They get handed off to a customer success team and sometimes that's not so smooth. Customers ask, "Why do I have to tell you my whole life story again?" Then, customer success might see an up-sell opportunity, but that goes to another account management department. It becomes awkward yet again. How do we mitigate that?

As the future B2B sales force moves away from selling, sales will be equipped and have processes in place to be much better at acquiring information about new accounts. They will have to be better at documenting and recording what they do. But it will all be driven by marketing because marketing will understand the importance of preparing for what's next in the cycle.

So what happens to the sales profession and the distribution of Forrester Research's four sales archetypes (order taker, explainer, navigator, and consultant)?

There's going to be a change in the mix of sales archetypes in most organizations. The one most at risk is the order taker. He's not providing much value because now customers can place an order themselves. Most companies will focus on having as many consulting and navigating sales reps. They help drive the long-term relationships that maximize customer lifetime value. They help buyers to buy. Not selling, selling, selling, but helping, helping, helping. I think you'll start to see training to encourage that type of behavior. I even think companies are thinking about the words *selling* and *sales force* and maybe, over time, moving away from those terms.

Ultimately, I think these are exciting times to be in B2B marketing. We've suffered from being seen as sales support. Now the recognition is there that we must be more strategic.

Prediction #4—Academia Catches Up

Most universities offer degrees in marketing, accounting, finance, and even business management. Have you ever seen a degree in sales? For marketing, although it's a popular degree, it's been primarily consumer-focused. Remember the 4 Ps: product, promotion, place, and price? We think that will change.

We believe universities and other progressive institutions will soon view formal B2B programs as essential for preparing students for the real world. Here are a few examples of this trend currently at work.

- Students enrolled in University of Central Florida's undergraduate marketing program can take their Professional Selling Program, which offers an opportunity to participate in a national B2B selling competition.

- Bend Poly, an innovative digital marketing program out of Bend, Oregon, gives students relevant skills and exposure to real-world business projects.

- Claremont McKenna College in Southern California, currently ranked 18 on *Forbes'* list of "America's Top Colleges," has a Silicon Valley Program, where, much like a study-abroad program, students get course credit for a semester-long internship at companies like eBay and Intuit.

Expect to see marketing programs continue to modernize while sales programs become more common and all business programs continue to train students in advanced technologies and tools. About two dozen U.S. universities offer bachelor's degrees in data science or data analytics, but more will offer similar and purely business-focused degrees in these areas as data becomes more critical to business success.

Prediction #5—Marketing Compensation Gets Tied to Pipeline

This is a very scary concept to most marketers, who think of lead generation as their only responsibility and pipeline as the responsibility of sales. Because we've made such a big deal about pipeline being the common metric in your alignment efforts, we think marketing has to walk the walk.

We're not saying that marketers should be given a lower base pay and a completely variable compensation package like sales reps. We are saying that marketing should have more of their variable pay based on pipeline. This will *really* get marketing involved with sales and it will give sales a new level of respect for marketing.

At InsideView we have 100 percent transparency on our quarterly objectives, company wide. Sales can see what pipeline marketing has signed up for and how they perform against their goals. This goes beyond demand-generation roles—it's across every role in marketing, from product marketing to competitive analysis to public relations, and more.

Another compensation-based concept we're starting to hear more about—and agree with—is team revenue. In a team-revenue model, a portion of each sales rep's quota is the responsibility of marketing. It goes one step beyond pipeline and ties directly to quota attainment, so marketing is incented to work closely with each rep to the point they can actually quantify their direct impact on that rep's quota. It's definitely a bleeding-edge concept, but we expect to hear more progressive companies using it to build even stronger bonds of alignment between their sales and marketing teams.

Prediction #6—Account-Based Everything Becomes a Top Priority

Your business processes are undergoing major shifts and how you approach selling will be one of the most dramatic. At many companies, sales now follows up on leads based on the lead score. Scoring is typically based on things like emails opened and assets downloaded and, regardless of the contact's title or the account's firmographics, they're all scored the same. It generally doesn't consider the attributes of the whole account, such as revenue, total number of employees, or number of employees who opened your email.

An account-based model weights accounts on how likely they are to buy from you. When sales starts to reach out, their first interaction is based on the details of the account. The first call isn't about the white paper they downloaded; it's about the challenges they are facing.

InsideView hosted a webinar featuring two account-based marketing experts, Megan Heuer, VP and head of research at SiriusDecisions, and Jon Miller, CEO at Engagio, which makes software to help companies with complex enterprise sales. We ended up calling the topic "account-based everything," because it's not just marketing or selling; it's the entire approach.

An account-based model forces you to look at your current processes through a new lens, particularly when it comes to defining your ideal customers. By starting there, sales and marketing can align to determine how they need to work together to capture those customers. It helps align everyone involved in the deal cycle: sales, sales development, customer success, marketing, and more. In fact, when asked about common pitfalls, Jon said, "The worst outcome is if marketing puts half its effort into named accounts, but sales is only expecting to get 30 percent of its pipeline in revenue from those accounts." Megan and Jon both agreed that misalignment is at the center of most failures in account-based sales and marketing.

How you measure your account-based program's success is also critical. Jon offered five key metrics:

1. Coverage: Do you have sufficient contacts and account plans for each target account?

2. Awareness: Are the target accounts aware of your company and its solutions?

3. Engagement: Are the right people at the accounts spending time with your company and is that engagement going up over time?

4. Program impact: Are marketing programs matching the target accounts, and are they having a long-term effect?

5. Influence: How are activities improving sales outcomes, such as deal velocity, win rates, average contract values, retentions, and net promoter scores?

It takes time for metrics to show results, but you should start to measure awareness and account coverage before you even begin targeting accounts.

At this point, you might be thinking, "Huh? You want me to align and revamp how we go to market?" Yes, because one can jumpstart the other.

Do It Right: Build an Account-Based Engagement Model

Matt Amundson is senior director of sales development at EverString, developers of predictive analytics software for sales and marketing. He's an expert on account-based selling, and he runs the account-based selling process at EverString. Here's what he had to say:

"Moving to an account-based sales and marketing model helps you create a meaningful first conversation. We now use triggers that we've discovered about the account to tailor that first message, rather than generically trying to engage. The difference is that you stop focusing on all leads and start focusing on leads that are likely to want to buy from you. That requires that you know who that is, so you need to define your target markets and personas.

"Next, you need to have the right metrics in place. You're no longer looking at leads, you're looking at engagement. How you measure engagement is up to you, but you're forcing yourself to shift away from traditional metrics and toward account-based metrics. For example, don't look at how many times a lead has visited your website, look at how many times anyone from XYZ Corporation has visited your website.

"Next, get marketing involved much deeper into the pipeline. This is a key aspect of alignment, so it works well with account-based selling. You're going to need a lot more account-specific content from marketing, but marketing is also going to learn and be able to create highly effective campaigns that pull in more leads from the right accounts.

(Continued)

(Continued)
Just like alignment, however, moving to account-based selling is jarring. Most people aren't familiar with it and fewer yet have ever done it at a company level.

"Sales will see a lot fewer leads and they'll schedule a lot fewer meetings. That's scary. But they'll quickly see that these are much better meetings. It also changes how sales has to approach a lead. We're frequently talking to accounts that don't yet know that they need our products. That forces us to change our entire sales process from selling to evangelizing. Sales can no longer just disqualify a lead because they're not interested. They have to take the time to make them interested.

"On the marketing side, they're forced to generate a lot more content that's much more tailored than before. It feels like more work, but it's really focusing on specific accounts and giving them what they need.

"Your first step is to figure out who your targets really are and everyone has to be in agreement."

Prediction #7—Customer Data Strategy Rises in Importance

Exploding data volumes, new technologies, and new data will continue to change everything. That's a mouthful, but it's true. Yesterday, we were impressed with web analytics. Tomorrow, we'll be getting data from drones, from smart watches, and from self-driving cars—and plenty of other things we haven't even dreamed of yet!

Millennials are notoriously comfortable with their lack of digital privacy. This will extend to their careers and the lines between their personal data and work data will blur. Today, if you're selling sheet metal, for example, you probably don't care what's on a prospect's Facebook page, but soon you'll adjust your targeting and your messaging based not only on attributes such as a buyer's product needs, but also on their past vacation destinations, their affinity for Formula One racing, and their recent installation of a swimming pool. In an account-based world, you'll further connect the data linking an opportunity's decision makers to help you be more effective. And that's all before you ever even meet the buyers.

This data is out there and you'll be using more of it to better target, engage, and sell. But thinking strategically and maintaining your data will become more critical than ever. As you trim your tech stack, if you haven't already done so, start thinking about trimming your data as well. Our example of vacation destinations may not correlate with your win rates, so evaluate if you even need it. We will see more services and more tools related only to data, data maintenance, and data hygiene in the next few years, and you will be using them. Everyone knows that data is the lifeblood of the modern business, so start thinking about your data's cholesterol levels.

Advancing technologies are driving this need for data strategy. Paul Holland is a general partner at Foundation Capital, a venture capital firm and an investor in InsideView. He also sits on InsideView's board. Paul sees plenty of cutting-edge technology companies, so he has a good view of what's coming next and how the approach to sales and marketing is changing. One area to watch is where challenges are growing enough to support new industries. In many cases, that is where you find B2B sales and marketing making radical shifts.

"We're seeing entirely new models of customer engagement, where B2B companies are proud to say that they have no sales team and no lead generation," Paul says. "Companies like Slack (which manages team communications) and GitHub (which helps companies design, build, and ship software) have products that are so good they don't need to be sold in the traditional sense. The only thing they do is upsell companies to pay for enterprise features. These companies take away all of the friction. The product sells itself. There's no need for an amazing marketing program or even sales people."

This is the eventual future, where artificial intelligence and bots become so smart and capture so much diverse data, that machines do the marketing and selling. For now, however, successful *traditional* companies are sprinting ahead because they're recognizing the need for widespread alignment.

"The successful companies today run like finely tuned machines," Paul adds. "Sales is well served by marketing. Marketing programs are executed well. Both teams use a common dataset, helping them manage to the same information. They also have a good culture. All of that comes together to help a company make its number. If you don't have those things, the poor execution will show up and the value of a company will diminish."

Technology that hasn't even been thought of yet is right around the corner and with it will come even more data. You'll soon attend sales meetings in virtual reality, watching and giving presentations without leaving your living room. You'll soon ask Apple's Siri or IBM's Watson to give you the top three target personas for your next campaign, and then to email customized content instantly to your matching contacts. And these aren't 10 or even 5 years away. These types of advances will happen within a few quarters.

But the march of technology is also a mess for sales and marketing. There are thousands of tools available now and more tech companies are constantly launching more tools, each with their own fountains of data. That's probably never going to change. What will happen is consolidation. It's the natural life cycle of technology, and it's going to happen very quickly. We're already hearing from our own customers who are eliminating tools and we've done it ourselves. All of these point solutions will be rolled up as features into customer relationship management (CRM) and marketing automation, which will make your tech stack a little bit less messy.

Expect Alignment to Continue Its Expansion

Sales and marketing alignment is trending for several reasons. First, misalignment has become an obvious drag on growth. There are numerous data points to support this. Second, grabbing the customer's attention is getting more difficult as they continue to control their own journey more directly. Finally, the benefits of alignment are well documented, proven, and substantial. Once sales and marketing alignment becomes the status quo, expect company-wide alignment to become the natural next step.

We've talked about sales and marketing as the tip of the spear. What's behind that metaphor, literally, is the rest of the company. If you can align sales and marketing, which engages the customer and drives growth, the rest of the company will fall in line. IT will want to align with marketing, finance and legal will want to align with sales, and sales will want to align with customer service. It's a positive trend in the right direction, and it's just beginning.

We have our Smarketing Meetings, so why not Sproduct Meetings? OK, that's too hard to say, but why not get operations and sales and marketing aligned and working towards growth, together? Peers in other departments are asking, "How can we help?" and "How can we do this *together?*" We are getting attention for the advances we're making with alignment, and it's not only for the growth benefits, but also for the day-to-day benefits of making this a better place to work. For everyone.

True leadership isn't just you doing something and going in new directions, it's getting people to take the journey with you. Sure, sometimes you'll fall on your face, but get up and you'll be smarter the next time.

Prepare Your Team for Tomorrow, but Start Cheering Them on Today

Change is inevitable, but preparing for that change is optional. It's up to you to get your teams ready by keeping them focused, motivated, and encouraged as change happens. The fear of change can cause sales and marketing team members to pause and look over their shoulders for what could be changing next. It's up to us as leaders to provide the climate for them to feel supported through the changes and feel comfortable enough to be looking ahead with optimism.

Salespeople and marketers themselves are changing too. As the leader, you need to recognize and adjust your leadership style. Part of being a leader though drastic change is to motivate, and we are seeing aligned sales and marketing becoming the de facto motivators for their entire companies.

Both sales and marketing have to be the cheerleaders for moving to alignment today and reaping the benefits of alignment tomorrow. Andrea knows her sales team at InsideView believes in alignment, but there are still discouraging setbacks, missteps, and challenges. When she's helping someone on her team work through a challenge, she likes to recognize the difficulty, but realizes they can get through it. "Someone is going to figure this out. Why can't it be you? Why can't it be us?" she likes to say.

Being the cheerleader doesn't mean everything is always rosy. You have to know within yourself that it's OK to be wrong or to not know. You have to teach your team it's OK to talk about missed targets and missed goals; it's OK to talk about failure. Being a good leader means turning those misses into learning opportunities, and recognizing that you lose credibility when you say that everything is great when it obviously isn't. Failing is OK if you fail forward and learn from the experience, but also try to not repeat the failure.

As you push alignment forward and encounter the inevitable bumps, start to ask yourself why you can't be the one to reach across the aisle. Force yourself to be the person who raises issues, recognizes and addresses tension, and eliminates the undercurrents of frustration and mistrust that can derail your efforts.

This is going to be true as you evaluate your culture, adjust your processes, improve your leadership skills, and optimize your technology. Your future depends on your ability to bring people together and to look for solutions, but it also depends on your ability to recognize what's coming and prepare for where your business goes.

The role of sales and marketing is changing, so the role of the sales and marketing *leader* will need to change as well.

If You Do Nothing Else About Alignment, Do These Things

Look in the mirror, assess where you are, and ask if you're willing to put yourself out there. What are you waiting for? Get started.

1. Talk to your immediate team members and garner their support

2. Talk to your CEO and get them to agree to senior leadership support

3. Meet with your sales or marketing counterpart, even if you are hesitant about their response.

4. Give them this book. Share it with your teams. And talk about the concepts, together. The more people involved, the faster you'll get there and reap the results.

5. Let us know how it goes! #AlignedtoAchieve

Acknowledgments

This book reflects the combined efforts of not only us as authors, but also our *village* of colleagues, mentors, interviewees, analysts, consultants, journalists, thought leaders, and others who helped to inform, guide, and assist us. Their wisdom and experience continues to advance our thinking on sales and marketing alignment, and vastly improved the content of this book.

We'd like to thank the dozens of professionals who contributed their valuable time and insights by indulging our questions and probing during interviews and conversations: Matt Amundson, Alvina Antar, Cari Baldwin, Kerry Barrett, John Barrows, Tracy Birdsall, Scott Brinker, Sharmila Chatterjee, Grad Conn, Esther Costa, Kim DeCarlis, Jim Dickie, Jon Donlon, Christelle Flauhaux, Jay Fulcher, Ashu Garg, Barb Giamanco, Sebastian Grady, Howard Gwin, Elisabeth Hawkins, Megan Heuer, Paul Holland, Chad Lindsay, Nancy Malkin, Jon Miller, Nancy Nardin, Peter O'Neill, Lia Ottaviano, Laura Ramos, BVR Mohan Reddy, Robin Saitz, Tamara Schenk, Jason Seeba, Mary Shea, Alex Shipillo, Will Spendlove, Kelly Steckelberg, Tim Thorpe, Rob Wahbe, Adrienne Weissman, Fredrik Winterlind, and Lori Wizdo.

We'd also like to recognize several of our InsideView colleagues who contributed their time and effort to make this book a reality: Stefan Burak, Vince Canobbio, Molly Davis, Megan McConnell, Ben VanderVeen, Heidi Vasconi, Kristine Webb and—most notably—Jason Rushin, without whom this book wouldn't have been possible.

Finally, we'd like to thank Umberto Milletti, InsideView's CEO and the driving force behind the company's sales and marketing alignment efforts. His guidance and leadership, along with his support for this book, inspired us to write it in the first place.

Index